THOUGHT
PRISON

THOUGHT PRISON

The fundamental nature of political correctness

Bruce G Charlton

University of Buckingham Press

First published in Great Britain in 2011 by

The University of Buckingham Press

Yeomanry House

Hunter Street

Buckingham MK18 1EG

CIP catalogue record for this book is available at the British Library

ISBN 978 0 9563953 45

Biography

Bruce G Charlton is Visiting Professor of Theoretical Medicine at the University of Buckingham. Bruce has an unusually broad intellectual experience: he graduated with honours from the Newcastle Medical School, took a doctorate at the Medical Research Council Neuroendocrinology Unit, and did postgraduate training in psychiatry and public health. He has held university lectureships in physiology, anatomy, epidemiology and psychology; and holds a Masters degree in English literature from Durham. Professor Charlton has published considerably more than two hundred scientific papers and academic essays in these fields, and contributed journalism to UK national broadsheets and weekly magazines.

Acknowledgements

The ideas and analysis of this book are indebted to a vast number of people over three decades, and of course to experience: personal, professional and political.

But the major positive influences on my thesis are threefold: JRR Tolkien, CS Lewis and Blessed Father Seraphim Rose (1934-1982) – a US-born Hieromonk of Platina, California in the Russian Orthodox Church Outside Russia whose essays, books, translations, collections and personal example are the most profound of antidotes to PC.

A special 'thank you' goes to a group of thoughtful regular (and often pseudonymous) commenters at my blog *Bruce Charlton's Miscellany*, where these ideas were first formulated and drafted; and to John Granger (a.k.a. The Hogwarts Professor) for his clarifying exposition of the *Harry Potter* series of novels by JK Rowling.

James Kalb's writings on 'Liberalism' (meaning the same phenomenon which I chose to call Political Correctness) are the most insightful of any that I know. Indeed, *Thought Prison* was written under considerable 'anxiety of influence' with respect to Jim! I thank him for his cover comments; and whole-heartedly recommend his book *The Tyranny of Liberalism* to any who wish to follow my analysis to a deeper level.

My family are what remind me that, although political correctness now extends its tentacles *almost* everywhere, there are still islands of soul and sanity – so this book is dedicated to Fraser, Gill, Billy and Nancy.

Contents

Why I use the term Political Correctness, instead of Liberalism or Socialism?

The reasons include:

1. The confusion over what 'liberalism' means - to some a free marketeer, to others a socialist. My definition of political correctness is broad and includes most mainstream conservatives, libertarians and anarchists; who are nowadays all significantly PC.

2. Differences in usage between the UK and US: in the UK the Liberals are a strange mixture of business- and farming-friendly Centrists with pacifist Leftists of an upper middle class type; in the US Liberals are the furthest Left of mainstream political ideologies.

3. That although PC clearly evolved from what is in the UK called socialism, and in the US called liberalism; PC is the outcome of a distinctive 'turn' in Leftist politics, which became obvious in the mid-1960s. In its striking, explicit, surface features PC is something new under the sun, never before seen in history.

4. Leftist political groups have, over the years, called themselves Communist, Socialist, Labour, Social Democrat, Liberal Democrat, Democrat and various other names – but none of these have become dominant, and none are fully inclusive of Leftism.

5. The dawning realization that the phenomena collected together under the jokey term 'political correctness' was a vastly more robust and malignant thing than I had ever imagined.

*

So that what seemed either silly or trivial or both, will end by destroying that modernity which made PC possible in the first place.

Yet we can perceive now, in advance of all this, that even when PC is utterly swept-away it will be blind to what has happened, and to what it had done. PC will always see itself as being on the side of the angels, whatever its outcome may be.

*

It is a truly amazing thing, this political correctness; something so paltry, so puny, so soft - yet wreaking such devastation while rendering the devastation imperceptible.

It seemed, therefore, worth discussing under its new name, as a phenomenon not truly new at its deepest level - but new in its combination of idealistic, delusional subjectivism with deadly, plodding bureaucracy.

Introduction

Political correctness (PC) is the dominant ideology of the Western intellectual world – PC is what the West has instead of a religion.

PC is a thing of the political Left in its origins and central constituency, yet has in recent decades been embraced by the mainstream political Right and Centre. Political correctness therefore represents the triumph of the Left.

Nonetheless, political correctness very obviously violates both common sense and logic, and is destructive of all that is good, beautiful and true.

So, at one and the same time, PC is marginal and mainstream, ridiculous and mandatory; crazy and normal.

This book explains how something so bizarre and wicked could become so ubiquitous and unremarkable.

*

Political correctness obviously dominates its core territory of politics, public administration (the civil service), law, education and (especially!) the mass media. But PC also substantially shapes everything else: foreign policy, the military, policing, the economy, health services, and personal life: the mating game, friendships and even family life.

Therefore political correctness is objectively totalitarian. That is to say comprehensively coercive of body and spirit, against human agency: anti-the soul.

Just as with the cruder totalitarianism of the mid-twentieth century, PC has created a population that lives in fear: fear of being denounced and losing everything – fear of committing (or indeed merely being accused-of) a thought crime or uttering a hate fact for which there is no defence; fear of the sanctions which range from social ostracism, through loss of job, financial penalties, up to directed mob violence and imprisonment.

Consequently the mass of people, especially those of status – with power and influence – have learned and internalized the constraints of political correctness, so that it is now something inside us, as well as pressing upon us. The shabbiness, lies and wickedness of PC permeate our very thought processes.

As if in illustration, this book has no specific examples of political correctness.

The reader must provide relevant instances from personal experience and unofficial knowledge.

Anyone unable to do this will be unmoved by my arguments.

*

So, political correctness is the ruling ideology of the West, and it is everywhere, so it cannot be attacked or overthrown without attacking and overthrowing pretty much everything. Political correctness is therefore *de facto* irrefutable, immovable, expansile in tendency... and yet, of course, as we all recognize, PC is self-destroying: achievement of its aims is common-sensically incompatible with its own survival.

*

Am I therefore suggesting that Western civilization is doomed? Yes, very probably it is doomed.

Can anything be done to prevent this, anything political perhaps? No – I don't think so.

So why am I bothering to write a book about it?

The answer is simple, but will strike most of my target audience of secular intellectuals as bizarre at best, nonsense at worst: the answer is so that some individuals may escape the general corruption and save their souls.

Because, PC is – more than anything else – destructive of the soul – proceeds, indeed, from the denial of the soul.

And if you don't know what I mean by this: Read On...

Political correctness no longer a joke...

When I first came across political correctness – which was the summer of 1981, inflicted on me by a social worker – I thought it was a bad joke.

Even in 1992, when I was in a Texas university humanities department for a month, and I saw the thing close-up and in full flight, it still seemed too obviously silly to take seriously.

Now, of course, the joke is on me: PC defines reality, and we all live and work at the whim of the advocates of PC, who could destroy the lives of any one of us at any moment, for any reason or for no reason whatsoever.

And they would feel good about doing it.

Escape from habituation into nihilism

Whence comes the sheer venom of PC?

How is it that people who *believe in nothing* (or, if they believe in anything, it is supposedly in tolerance, pacifism, 'relativism', social constructionism…stuff like that) – how come these people are so vicious?

I think it is because they fear that their own *pleasurable distractions* – their lifestyle choices – will be constrained or even taken-away by the opponents of PC.

And for the PC, pleasurable distraction is life itself.

*

I say this without a shred of exaggeration.

If you believe in nothing, if life can have no real objective meaning and all is socially constructed; then pleasure is *absolutely* necessary as an analgesic, and *distraction is the primary philosophical argument.*

The politically correct are nihilists, that is reality-deniers, and when there is no reality then the only positive is pleasure.

*

(Yet, is it *really* correct to say that the politically correct are nihilists, believing in nothing? Surely the opposite is true, that the most PC are precisely those who 'passionately' believe in things like multiculturalism, diversity, equality, world peace and so on? But the most PC really are nihilists in that they deny the reality of reality. For political correctness there is no objective underlying reality. For PC, truth is a social construct: subjective, malleable, evolving. So PC does not discover truth, it *makes* truth; does not fit itself to reality but *creates* reality via the shaping of discourse. Since nihilism is precisely the denial of truth and reality; the politically correct are certainly nihilists by a strict and accurate definition.)

*

But all pleasures are up-against *habituation*: on repetition, pleasures lose their effect.

This is basic biology, and unavoidable.

Habituation is the driving force of modernity – the drive behind neophilia (love of the new), the drive behind fashion, the drive behind the leading edge of political correctness.

Habituation rules because without *effective* stimuli, without perpetual *novelty*, modernity is lost – and without pleasurable distraction modernity will be confronted by the void; and for a nihilist the void is no joke, but is indeed the only reality.

*

For the nihilist, 'the real' is an illusion, illusion the only reality: therefore to live is necessarily to be deluded.

There is no truth, merely a choice between delusions (some more gratifying than others, some more altruistic than others).

3

Unconstrained by unitary truth, the choice of 'realities' (that is of delusions) is potentially infinite.

Political correctness is a process of deliberately self-induced delusion (ideally, to the point of self-forgetting the act of choosing a delusion).

Thus the need for change (neophilia) which characterizes modernity: the need constantly to break boundaries, to transgress, always in search of novel hence more-powerful stimuli to connect us with the insubstantial world.

Under modernity, humans are jaded by pleasures repeated.

We are all decadent, all Caligulas now.

*

So, any who challenge the escalation of stimuli, the freedom to transgress, the breaking of bounds, the primacy of lifestyle, the mix of populations, the imagined possibility of the exotic...

Any who assert the eternal, the unchanging, who seek to limit the potential of the future (even by word – especially by word)…

Any who aim to ground life on truth, on reality…

Any and all such persons or groups *strike at the roots of vitality*.

And for PC vitality is all and only.

Even as such a *reactionary* speaks, or is read, or watched – as he *invades* PC discourse – the politically correct can feel their *life draining away*, can sense the world receding, can perceive the delusional world crumbling, the void yawning.

Hence the viciousness, the panicked attack using anything to hand which might work: *ad hominem* inventions (immediately believed as facts), fantasied motivations, lies of any and every kind and even violence (at second hand – regretted, maybe, but neither wholly condemned nor effectively prevented).

For the PC it is vitally necessary to control discourse, to exclude all hostile communications if possible, immediately to *stop* them if they break through. There can be no delay – effective dissent must be shouted-down, mocked, vilified, *shut-up*; the politically correct must switch-off, turn-away, gabble and gossip to drown or distract from the content of hostile discourse; instruct, direct and unleash the mob – then begin again to rebuild the thought prison of PC discourse by their own words, in their own image.

*

The venom of the politically correct is the venom of a person faced by the extinction of those pleasurable distractions *upon which they rely utterly to keep themselves going*: the ever-expanding choice of favourite food; the anticipated holidays anywhere; the unbounded potential novelties of sex, picking and mixing among an un-endingly growing, whirling and recombining of persons, cultures and ideas; the experimentation with drinks and (maybe) drugs; fantastic hopes for these to be facilitated by world peace, harmony, abolition of poverty, blendings: in sum, the infinite *possibilities* of the future, and the hope of pleasures so overwhelming and utterly absorbing as to extinguish all concerns relating to meaninglessness or lack of purpose: strong enough to *delete* self-consciousness.

*

The more extreme, the less realistic, the greater the delusional psychoticism of the PC dream – the greater its fragility; and the greater the loathing of anyone who threatens to shatter it.

*

Against such reactionaries *anything* is permitted – restrained only by the danger of evoking such an extreme of self-disgust, of demoralization, as to shatter the dream oneself.

This is the danger faced by the intellectual elite – that one day they will behave such that they will destroy their own delusions of themselves.

Then there will be nowhere for them to turn.

Nowhere at all.

The irrationality of PC

Logic is extremely dangerous to political correctness, since its basic survival mechanism is one of continual revolution, continual attack, continual ground-shifting.

Logic, by contrast, presupposes an eternal and unchanging standard.

Political correctness *hates* that kind of thing…

*

Anyone who looks as if they might get PC to stay in one place and argue things out, fully and at leisure, without changing the subject, without descending into denunciation, is therefore exceedingly dangerous.

PC (being psychotic, hence thought-disordered; constituted by fragmentary and disconnected ideas linked only by a general trend) *cannot* argue rationally for anything longer than a sound bite segment.

And if, *by accident*, PC starts arguing rationally, and sustains this for more than a very short time – especially if the process begins to link one thing with another and action with consequence – then it simply stops being PC.

*

When a thoroughly PC intellectual senses this happening, senses that he is being backed-into-a corner where he will need to engage in a properly rational discourse, or senses that the discussion is spreading into other fields and making *connections* – then (according to the rules of PC) *anything* is permitted if it enables escape from this emergency situation.

Even violence. PC-sanctioned Leftist or privileged-'minority' gangs are allowed, indeed tacitly *encouraged*, to shout-down, intimidate, silence, assault, and if necessary *kill* non-PC speakers or writers or organizers – to ensure that any dangerous process of sustained and connected interchange cannot get started, cannot be imposed on the public discourse.

This pattern of coercively *shutting-down* anti-PC voices has been repeated on college campuses and in public spaces innumerable times since PC began its dominance in the mid 1960s.

*

It is forbidden for the politically correct to *engage* with the enemy.

Any individual or organization which does engage with the enemies of PC will itself immediately and irrevocably be classified as *an enemy of PC*.

*

The requirement to avoid rational engagement is not merely to avoid the 'risk' of being out-argued or proved wrong – it is because rational debate itself cannot be allowed to happen.

To discourse rationally is for PC to die.

On the spot.

Imaginary enemies preferred

Since George Orwell, we have all understood the importance of enemies to progressive politics.

Without enemies the Left cannot function – since it is based upon unending change; permanent revolution, subversion and inversion; incessant destruction of the past and the fixed.

Leftism is based on utter absorption in the battle of overcoming resistance to itself, and avoidance of any consideration about where all this is going and why.

The Left is all tactics and no strategy.

*

(The Left has no strategy because for the Left there is no *reality*, there is nothing that really matters outwith human communications, no goal that is stable, no thing actual to aim-for. By contrast the reactionary religious Right do not *need* enemies, since they believe in reality and The Good; and therefore have a real goal toward which they strive and which they really want to reach. If there are no enemies blocking the path to this goal, then so much the better. The religious Right may *in practice* use enemies tactically, or for self-motivation, in much the same way as the Left; but reactionaries do not *require* enemies.)

*

On the one hand political correctness *needs* enemies, yet on the other hand never can *engage* with those enemies; the enemies serve a vital but purely symbolic function.

Therefore fantasy enemies are the best ones for PC – racist white nationalist organizations; for example.

Such fictional groups have been constructed by the media over several decades, depicted frequently and repetitively in movies and TV programs and continually referenced in the press and online.

Drip, drip, drip – inventions treated as facts.

*

Creative depictions are treated as if they were real, immediate and terrifying threats; justifying perpetual consciousness-raising, continual suppression and distortion of important information, expansile rules and laws, insidious totalitarian repression and a state of constant revolution.

The enemies *seem* real, and that is enough.

*

And the really great thing about *fictional* enemies – just like the compassion-groups of PC: such as foreign ethnics, animals, the environment – is that they cannot talk back.

Indeed they cannot talk at all: except to say whatever you put into their mouths.

Imaginary enemies are under control.

*

(Of course there is a danger that fictional enemies will become real; that the imaginary depictions will, sooner-or-later put ideas into heads, and will attract people to fill the ready-made *niche* that PC propaganda has itself created. Real, human, talking and autonomously-acting enemies occupying their most loathed and feared fantasy representations constitutes an ultimate nightmare for political correctness.)

Why is PC so shallow, flippant and reckless?

The short answer is because PC intellectuals do not think intellectual discourse is serious.

And they do not think intellectual discourse is serious because they do not think that *anything* is serious, because they are 'relativistic' nihilists (social constructivists) who do not believe in the eternal, unchangeable, objective nature of reality and who will soon be dead, anyway, so why bother?

*

PC tactical retreats in the face of serious rational discourse:

1 Who knows?

Nothing is certain. Subjective factors interfere everywhere. It is dangerous to claim certainty when none is to be had. Maybe you are *correct*, deep down, but as we never can know *reality* then we will never know for sure...

In the meantime I might as well enjoy myself, or at least avoid unnecessary suffering.

*

2. Nothing is really real.

Well, ultimately nothing is real anyway; so whether you are more correct than I am doesn't really matter, because the universe is ultimately chaos; any apparent order is just a random blip on the road to entropy…

In the meantime I might as well enjoy myself, or at least avoid unnecessary suffering.

*

3. It will last my time.

Maybe you *are* correct, maybe my views will indeed lead to disaster, maybe currently-promoted behaviour is not sustainable or will destroy itself – but all that matters is that things keep going just long enough until I am gone. After all, when I am dead I won't know anything about it either way…

In the meantime I might as well enjoy myself, or at least avoid unnecessary suffering.

*

4. Death will put an end to it.

Even if things do not last my time, *even if* things do become awful – *even if* they become *intolerable* – since the 'immortal soul' is a childish fiction, death will put an end to my misery – so I can always escape by suicide…

In the meantime I might as well enjoy myself, or at least avoid unnecessary suffering.

*

13

Atheism and nihilism therefore serve as a *crutch* to the politically correct elite.

Political correctness, the intellectual elite and the mass media

PC depends upon at least two necessary (although not sufficient) conditions: an intellectual ruling class and a large and effective mass media.

The intellectual ruling elite are necessary because *only they* have the disposition for abstraction, the preference to regard ideas as realer than experience (because PC 'reality' is socially constructed), and the tendency to privilege ideas even (or especially) when they are in conflict with commonsense observation.

The mass media are necessary because the media constitute the discourse – the cognitive process, the mode of thinking – of modern societies.

*

Political correctness is (roughly) a mixture of bureaucratic Old Left and subjective New Left, the interspersion of a system of communist/ Fabian totalitarian central planning with irruptions of counter-cultural hedonism.

*

15

The main difference between the late Soviet Union in the Brezhnev era and political correctness in the West, is therefore the presence of a mass media.

In the old Soviet Union the media were instruments of state propaganda; they were dull, people didn't pay much attention to them, and the quantity of media output was anyway kept low (because the media content was controlled and checked, item by item).

In the modern West, by contrast, the mass media are vast, primarily attention-grabbing, and still growing; media content is vivid and varied; and the subject matter is controlled only by self-censorship.

The mass media and the memory hole

Modern Western humanity is addicted to the mass media for its near infinite provision of attention-grabbing novelty, the stimulation of which provides vital distraction from awareness of the nihilistic void underlying mainstream secular discourse.

The mass media is necessary to the dominance of political correctness, and itself defines the nature of modern discourse: itself embodies and imposes the mode of thinking which enables political correctness.

*

The way in which the media can put disapproved-of news 'down the memory hole' *simply by refraining from mentioning it*, provides an important insight into the nature of modern discourse.

Modern 'reality' is only *that which is in the media now*; this is the price paid for so much media content of such an attention-grabbing ability.

So much time is now expended by the addicted citizenry on acquiring 'news' that each day the new-news is poured-in, and the old-news is – by this – pushed-out.

When each day begins with the mind a clean slate – prepared and expecting to be written-upon, *then* the media control what is in people's minds – control the past, the present and (speculations about) the future.

To keep-up with the flood of news/ opinion/ analysis/ gossip means that we must accord news priority over history; and the old can only survive by being continually re-made as new.

(Even 'history' is only real when it is made news. Old history is regarded as dull, obsolete and most likely as evil and dangerous – since old history is never politically correct. Supposing someone was actually to believe it!)

This process is critical to modernity, because the media process is *intrinsically devaluing of the past* – of past people, opinions and facts.

*

This is indeed a key to the *inversions* of political correctness.

The casual, routine, un-argued assumption of *the superiority of the current* is an assumption which itself derives from the nihilism that reality is 'socially constructed'; that *the only* 'reality' is an aggregation of here-and-now mental contents.

This pragmatic fact of modern life is critical to the ability of the PC elites to retain their claim to moral authority; because via the media the intellectual class is able continually to re-make morality, truth and aesthetics.

What is current in the media is definitive. Sin can be made into virtue, virtue into sin; propaganda can be made into truth, truth into propaganda; beauty can be reframed as *Kitsch* and ugliness celebrated as beauty.

*

When the only reality is subjective, and subjectivity is filled with the media, and the intellectual elites fill the media: then *the intellectual class define reality.*

Fashion and PC

The characteristic *modus operandi* of political correctness is *fashion*.

*

Fashion is not coercive, but everybody follows it (or, at least, everybody who 'matters').

So fashion is 'harmonious' – we all cooperate to make fashion, and we do so as a result of – well – *propaganda* I suppose. It is *discourse* (mostly the mass media) which informs and persuades people to follow fashion.

*

People follow fashion (merely) to belong; but to follow fashion *is* to belong; and the only (non-coercive) sanction is that *if* you do *not* follow fashion *then* you do *not* belong.

*

It all seems very mild; but it turns-out that this combination of reward and sanction is sufficient under modern conditions to ensure the domination of fashion everywhere and in everything.

*

So fashion is social harmony, implemented non-coercively via discourse – and of course fashion provides *novelty*.

Therefore, unlike traditional societies in which social harmony is static, often coercive and aspires to be eternal; and therefore has a tendency to be *boring* – fashion is dynamic and interesting because new and unfamiliar.

When we begin to get sick of fashion, and the novelty starts wearing-off, fashion can either become more extreme in the same direction, or else it can be inverted, or else a completely new fashion may be invented, or else a more-or-less-forgotten old fashion can be revived but with some twist, or several old fashions can be recombined.

*

Isn't fashion, therefore, an almost-exact analogy for the world to which PC aspires?

A world where everybody believes and wants the same thing – and so is harmonious and free from conflict and dangers; but also a world where the 'same thing' is continually changing (and evolving); and finally a world where all this is achieved (potentially) non-coercively by monopolistic control of discourse, of human communications.

Old Left – New Left

Perhaps the New Left 1960s counter-culture would have happened even without a mass media to report and record it?

Perhaps the children of the intellectual elite would still have rebelled against the dullness, boredom and alienation of modernity – even if they were not being sympathetically shown 'rebelling' on TV and in newspapers?

But without the mass media, the student revolutionaries, tenured radicals and crypto-communist fifth columnists would have had no lasting influence on national life.

Inchoate, hedonic rebellion is of itself fragmented, directionless and unsustainable.

It fizzles out.

*

But as it happened, the mass media was there, and the New Left did not fizzle out, but instead became integral to the mass media, which is to say that it became part of the West's cognitive processing.

*

Of course, the New Left cannot rationally be *integrated* with the Old Left; visceral hedonism cannot be fused with bureaucracy.

But they can be alternated in the human mind and in public discourse; and one can support the other.

*

The Old Left bureaucracy is the basis and mechanism of governance, that which holds-together modern society, that which allocates goods.

But Old Left bureaucracy on its own is psychologically *intolerable*, a dull and demotivating *machine* that grows itself but which is even less bearable for the bureaucrats than for their victims.

*

The New Left injected into this scenario counter-cultural but subjective qualities such as excitement (especially sexual and otherwise transgressive), 'purpose' (subversion, inversion), 'direction' (towards greater pleasure and less suffering), and variety (e.g. multi-culturalism, the 'other').

The New Left made the Old Left interesting and inspiring and idealistic for officials – but at a cost.

The cost of incoherence, fragmentation, delusional psychosis.

*

What was necessary to sustain the New Left countercultural spirit was that it became connected-with Old Left bureaucracy.

What was necessary to the Old Left organization was New Left engagement.

Result? Morally self-righteous bureaucracy.

Feel-good committees plus hype: a definition of PC.

*

Away from the mass media, the Old-New Left connection is intermittent and contradictory – in the mass media the connection is apparent and harmonious.

Nature of modern mass media

Some mistook the modern mass media for mere propaganda – it is indeed propaganda, but not merely.

Some mistook the modern mass media for mere entertainment – it is indeed entertainment, but not merely.

*

The old Eastern Bloc media were indeed merely propaganda – dull recitations of 'the party line'. Pure content.

Parts of the Western media have indeed been mere entertainment – 'chewing gum for the eyes'. Pure form.

*

But the *characteristic*, overall tendency of the Western mass media relates to both content and form: *entertaining propaganda*, and in truly vast quantities.

The Western mass media consists of competing institutions, which force it to be attention-grabbing, and drive its continual expansion.

The modern mass media is itself politically correct (staffed by the Leftist intellectual elite) and also the virtual arena for the thrilling perpetual sham warfare of political correctness against its mostly-fictional enemies.

Thought Prison

The battle ground of PC against reaction is the mass media; and this battle is itself a major – perhaps *the* major – content of the mass media.

*

So if it is asked: what exactly is it that the mass media propagandize for?

What would be the best answer?

The best answer is this: the mass media propagandize *the battle between PC and reaction*

(the battle between – 'as depicted' – on the one hand open-ended possibility and an expanding variety of novel lifestyles; and on the other hand dull, monochrome constraint; or, put more directly, the battle of universal compassion versus specific cruelty).

And in this battle the mass media is *intrinsically* on the side of PC, regardless of its specific content.

*

The battle of compassionate and fun PC versus boring and cruel reaction is depicted in the headlines and fine texture of news and documentary 'factual' mass media content – but also in the fictional, narrative content.

And of course these categories overlap – much of the purported factual content being actually fictional; much of the fictional stories and speculations actually being factual (where, by being treated as implicitly fictional and speculative, they become grist to the media mill rather than triggering real world responses).

And since the fictional (or factional) is most memorable – this is what is *remembered*. (If indeed *anything* is remembered.)

In the end there is a climate of made-reality, socially constructed reality; and the *really real* (eternal, unchanging) is not merely ignored and ridiculed but rendered incomprehensible – the ever–changing hourly experience of the mass media is what defines lived actuality.

Mass media as social cognition

The modern mass media both coerces and trains elite intellectual discourse – it does this by content, but more importantly by form.

It is from the media that the modern intellectual elite has learned *how to think*; has learned how to alternate between Old and New Left, between a baseline of rational bureaucracy and frequent irruptions of unbounded utopian idealism.

When to be rational, and when be passionate.

*

The mass media disciplines intellectuals and organizations who endanger political correctness: disciplines first by exclusion then by demonization – working like an inquisition by choosing and publicizing suitable anti-PC targets for aggression by 'the secular arm': organized Leftist direct action, rioting by approved groups, apparently-random acts by lone vigilantes – and so on.

The mass media identifies and locates reactionary targets for 'legitimate' aggression of many types; mostly verbal and procedural but also including violence.

And since these reactionary targets are seen as having willfully-provoked violence against themselves, the perpetrators of violence are exonerated from blame.

The immunity of PC to reason

The fragmentary structure of the modern mass media itself shapes discourse.

The underlying Leftism of personnel and of bureaucratic mechanisms (both are necessary) provides the default politically correct assumptions against which anti-PC intellectuals are requires to 'prove' their contentions.

But the fragmentary cognitive process of the mass media – bureaucracy alternating with counter-cultural idealism – makes rational proof systematically impossible.

The PC default is thus immune to any conceivable rational assault.

*

Once political correctness has been established, then the psychotic cognitive process of the media ensures that it is insulated from challenge, insulated from *reality*.

The modern intellectual elite are trained in this Old/ New Left PC cognitive style by the media, aspirants to elite status are screened and evaluated *primarily* on their competence, reliability and commitment to this mode of PC discourse – the ability to alternate bureaucratic proceduralism with irruptions of passionate, subjective conviction.

(Those aspiring to the PC elite are absolutely excluded from power if they are identified as being deficient in either respect, since both objective proceduralism and sustained subjectivism are equally fatal to political correctness.)

*

So – the necessary source of the PC delusion is the modern mass media, but this is not sufficient – PC also requires an intellectual ruling elite (and *not* a military or practical or religious ruling elite – such as prevailed in all historical societies, and prevails everywhere outside the developed world).

PC depends on both the mass media and an intellectual elite

If *either* the mass media *or* the intellectual elite were removed, then PC would collapse.

*

If the mass media were removed, then PC would collapse into Brezhnev-style centrally-planned communism (which would collapse from dullness and demotivation among the bureaucrats).

*

If the intellectual elite were removed from power, then the self-sustaining abstractions of PC would be experience-tested, subjected to common sense analysis and would collapse into reactionary politics: theocracy, nationalism or something akin to 'fascism'.

*

(But, due to the thought prison inhabited by the politically correct, they do not recognize this mutual dependence: PC intellectuals are suicidally-engaged in regulating, bureaucratizing and thereby damaging the mass media; the mass media suicidally agitate to discredit, disrupt and replace the ruling intellectual meritocracy.)

The impossibility of neutrality

Neutrality is a lynch pin of modern elite political thought.

Much of modern quasi-scientific social research is dedicated to demonstrating that some modern social system (law, education, the military) is not behaving neutrally. All that is required of such research is to show that (apparently, superficially) similar people of different sex, ethnicity or whatever are treated differently or have different outcomes, then the system stands discredited and requiring radical reform.

*

However, if it is actually *impossible* for an individual, an organization or a culture really to be neutral – then this debate takes on a different complexion altogether; because if impartiality is *unattainable*, then the debate would not *really* be about failure to attain the ideal of neutrality, but *actually* a debate over *who* should be favoured in situations that *must* be biased – one way or the other.

*

The ideal of impartiality in social systems probably derived from the ideal of law, in which the same system is (supposedly, ideally) applied to everyone – 'everyone' goes through the same basic process.

The same idea applies to bureaucracies, as described by Max Weber, in which administrators are required to devise and apply procedures impartially, treating operationally-similar cases as operationally-identical.

But in the real world there are major differences in the *application* both of the law and of bureaucratic procedures – differences such as: Who counts in practice as 'operationally similar': Who gets investigated? Who gets prosecuted? Who has penalties enforced on them? What actually happens to 'punished' people in practice? – and so on.

*

One classic political scenario nowadays involves someone (a radical) attacking a procedural system (such as the legal process, employment practice or educational evaluations) as being biased against such and such a group, while someone else (a libertarian or mainstream secular conservative) defends the system as being impartial-enough for the purposes.

The radical pretends to argue that impartiality is attainable but requires change, while *actually* seeking privileges for a particular group.

The libertarian/ conservative concedes that absolute impartiality is desirable and that the present system is therefore deficient; but argues (pragmatically) that the present system is *sufficiently good.*

The Left stands for Absolute Idealism and the Right for Functional Pragmatism…

*

Revealed as a mere pragmatist, the libertarian/ conservative always therefore gives some ground in the direction the idealistic radical is pushing, in the direction of 'perfection'; because any actually existing system is indeed imperfect, is indeed partial – of, at least, cannot be proven to be necessarily *im*-partial.

The Right is depicted as resisting improvement; therefore as a complacent – or more probably cruel – apologist for injustice.

Hence, under PC the existing (often historic) evaluation system is *always* overturned and revised in favour of the groups about which the radical was complaining.

That group which used to be privileged is now suppressed, and *vice versa*.

The proper question – whom to favour?

A truly reactionary perspective, by contrast, would *accept* the radical's implicit assumption that *one group or another must in reality be privileged*, and would challenge the radical on the grounds of *which* group ought to be privileged.

For example, if it is accepted that neutrality is impossible, then employment policy must favour *either* men *or* women – the proper question then becomes which is it *best* for employment policy to favour, and on what grounds?

For example, the organization of the military or care for young children will inevitably favour either men or women – the proper question to ask is: which is the most functionally-appropriate favoured group in each specific case?

(Clue: the correct answer is different for each of these two examples...)

When neutrality is rejected as impossible and undesirable, the focus of debate changes, and becomes a matter of determining the functional basis for favouring.

For instance, the Left usually favours 'social justice', the secular Right usually favours 'efficiency', the religious Right usually favours 'morality'.

*

One big advantage of acknowledging the inevitability of partiality is that this is what most people believe anyway and always have believed – in fact it is only a minority of the intellectual elite (libertarians and secular conservatives) who really believe in impartiality as a desirable and attainable goal of social systems.

But radicals, socialists, liberals and corrupt politicians are simply exploiting the failure to attain impartiality as a justification for imposing a *revolutionary inversion of values*.

Hence a belief in the ideal of neutrality unwittingly serves a radical and nihilistically-destructive agenda, since it actually leads to partiality in the opposite direction from that which is functional.

Assuming neutrality is impossible

Let us suppose that neutrality really is in practice impossible – just suppose that for a minute...

(I am personally very reluctant to admit this, I still find myself habitually defending the ideal of neutrality even after having seen-through it... But anyway, just *suppose* impartiality is an illusion and it really is *always* a choice between favouring one option, or the other. And naturally there will be *degrees* of favouring – but suppose that a significant degree of favouring really is inevitable.)

...Then if true this supposition would be a blow struck at the very core of rational*ism*, of modernity, of 'enlightenment'; of philosophical discourse, of science...

It would be to admit that *we have been deluded for centuries*, that we have been barking-up entirely the wrong tree, that we have been rendering our civilization helpless in the face of its opponents – worse, making our civilization abet its own downfall.

*

Just this simple error! – merely to suppose neutrality, impartiality of process, really was a possibility – and further that it really was desirable – instead of the fact (as it seems) that *always we must make a choice*.

Maybe it was this critical flaw in Western assumptions which led to our self-immolation?

But maybe, too, it was this same flaw which enabled the earlier rise of Western domination…

A double-edged sword.

Good causes and good intentions

It is necessary to recognize that political correctness is *not* well-intentioned; that it is merely, obsessively self-justifying: and that this is not-at-all the same thing as having good intentions.

*

Obviously, we are in a situation where explicit intentions are disconnected from observable outcomes. Yet since modernity broke-apart the moral universes of motivation and action (of faith and works) it cannot put them together again.

Political correctness therefore can find no satisfactory basis for moral action.

PC is therefore 'amoral' – which actually means immoral.

*

The moral universe of PC subsists on two distinct realities – good causes and good intentions, but never the twain can stay stuck-together.

(Note the lack of reference to good *outcomes*. Being wholly abstract, PC is indifferent to outcomes. 'Outcomes' are regarded as having no autonomous reality, but are merely seen as defined by abstract theory.)

*

A collection of PC-approved good causes confronts the individual; and it is up to him to manufacture his own subjective motivations for doing or not-doing them.

Or else he starts with his good intentions – his sympathies and desires – and manufactures more-or-less plausible symbolic acts by which their intentions are (supposedly) implemented; and it is up to the intellectual elite to manufacture some more-or-less plausible evidence that these acts flow from these intentions and are (or have potential to be) effective in the real world.

*

Somehow, intentions and causes never add-up to a morally cohesive world of acts; good-causes, good-intentions and virtuous-acts are continually being subverted, re-framed and re-interpreted by an ever-changing abstract interpretation.

When everything is interpretation, action is rendered hazardous, indeed unnecessary.

The bureaucrat and the media communicator (those who *do* nothing and *risk* nothing – but who interpret, and re-interpret reality for the masses) are the modern cultural exemplars: certainly not the heroic producer, maker and do-er (whose actions might, at any moment, be re-interpreted; and the erstwhile hero exposed as a modern villain.)

*

So, wretched inert submissiveness oscillates with arrogant but empty moral grandstanding.

The moral exemplar of PC ethics

Since progress is defined in terms of leaving-behind; the good is that which has left-behind the wicked; the wicked is that which has been left-behind by the movement of progress – the wicked are those people who *resist* the movement toward perfection.

*

If being left-behind is due to ignorance or incompetence, then that is okay – tolerated, even indulged and made the object of missionary work ('consciousness raising').

But if being left-behind is *willful*, if being left-behind is a matter of *refusing and resisting the next step in the march of moral progress* – then this is reaction.

So the moving-edge of progress continually leaves-behind newly-created reactionaries in its wake.

Which is useful for political correctness! Because hatred for reactionaries is its main under-pinning motivation – the urgent need to fight against reaction is what gets PC out-of-bed on cold winter mornings.

*

Under a system of PC, here and now in the West, the individual must adjust and adjust, again and again, to the widening wave of socially-defined progress – of moral denial, extrapolation and inversion.

Such repeated and unending adjustment is the individual's *non-negotiable moral duty* as a responsible adult member of the ruling elite.

So, the essence of PC morality is to keep-up with moral progress – to match one's inner motivation to the changing nature of socially-approved action (i.e. socially-approved by the ruling elite).

*

The moral exemplar, the 'hero' of PC ethics, is he whose convincingly-stated motivations are *slightly ahead* of the current state of socially-sanctioned actions, perceptibly 'advanced': further along in the direction that social progress is trending.

Nice work if you can get it.

Is anybody safe?

However, there is no safety for members of the ruling elite in a system of political correctness; anyone at all is susceptible to denunciation for any reason or no reason at any time. Whatever you may do, whatever willing you may show, status is contingent.

Since PC is a wave of moral 'progress' which leaves behind all previous moral standards and behaviours – there can be no accumulation of moral capital.

This applies to the ultra-PC just as much as to the openly reactionary.

*

(In this respect PC is more like communist than fascist totalitarianism: under fascism membership of and 'courageous loyalty to' the in-group usually brings safety from denunciation; but under communism anybody was vulnerable to denunciation – friends and enemies of the government alternated with bewildering rapidity: *nobody* was safe.)

Indeed, the PC elite seem *especially* vulnerable to denunciation – since they are under continuous scrutiny; it is hard to keep-up with the pace of change, and the change is so arbitrary; it is *very* difficult to suppress common sense 24/7.

The highest member of the PC elite is only a single *gaffe* away from disaster.

*

(Note: A 'gaffe' is when an elite PC intellectual momentarily forgets to lie.)

*

Under political correctness, you are only as good as today's match between your communications and the ever-changing societal symbols of virtue.

PC assumes that (as an elite intellectual) your motivations are bad unless proven good – and motivations cannot be proven.

You may advertise your good motivations relentlessly – daily, hourly – but you cannot ever prove conclusively, against hostile skepticism, that you are deep-down and overall a fully PC (hence decent) person.

(Not least because it is very unlikely that you *are* a decent person – after all, who is?).

*

All of this means that a politically correct social *diktat* can (from whatever cause – such as elite competition, the need for a scapegoat, or the whim of the media) arbitrarily decide at any time to stop giving you the benefit of the intrinsic doubt; and then you will be helpless, isolated, stripped of all moral status, a marked-man, a legitimate target of self-righteous aggression.

*

Because, after all, you *are* guilty – everybody is.

And scapegoats are sometimes necessary: tough luck that it happened to be you.

Safety for victim group members

For the intellectual elite there is no safety.

The only security is to be a member, a *representative* member, of an indulged group. That is a 'victim group' – a group which is a targeted beneficiary of PC.

(And even then you are vulnerable to denunciation by a higher status victim group.)

*

Victim group members can do more or less what they like – so long as they do not encroach on even-higher-status victim groups – and it is up-to the PC masters to make excuses for them, and find the support to enable them to continue.

*

As an indulged 'victim group' member your actions and motivations are tolerated and forgiven almost without limit – indeed, it is a test of PC that this be so.

The degree of PC moral status within the elite correlates closely with the degree of tolerance that you accord to victim groups – when tolerance becomes self-threatening quasi-suicidal *license*, we have entered the realms of PC 'sainthood'.

Life as a supervised game

But the news is not all good for victim group members – because as a PC-indulged victim you lack moral responsibility, which means you are treated as a child or an imbecile.

Kindly-treated, no doubt – nonetheless, to be regarded as a species of incompetent can sometimes be a source of... friction?

*

Exactly because you are not to blame for what you think or do, you are regarded as a victim of circumstances – and therefore you are not, and never can be, a moral agent or exemplar in your own right but only as *representative* of your victim group.

You are tolerated – with affection or with irritation – but you are not admired.

Because by merely *existing* you are regarded as special – therefore anything that you personally might think or do is automatically invalidated, rendered invisible.

*

As a member of an indulged victim group, your thoughts and behaviours are bracketed, encapsulated – set apart from that progressive moral actuality which is the preserve of the PC intellectual elite – an elite who *patronize* you in both senses of the word: in that they are your *patrons* who subsidize you and they treat you in a *paternal* fashion, as if you were their child.

*

(Patrons expect beneficiaries to be *grateful*. However, it has commonly been observed that patrons are in fact always hated. Do a man a good turn, and you will have an enemy for life. The patronized will not rest until they have expunged their sense of dependent gratitude in the cleansing act of biting-off the hand that has been stroking and feeding them.)

*

To be a member of a victim group under PC is to be a perpetual moral incompetent – susceptible to tantrums, not responsible for your actions, un-free, a product of uncontrollable impulse and overwhelming environment, an acted-upon *object* not a determining subject.

You may be flattered by praise – as teachers praise the efforts of a toddler: "Who's a *clever* boy, then!" – but under PC you are not, and never can be, one of the 'teachers'.

*

But how can PC intellectuals square this with the demands of the victim groups, and with their own guilty consciences?

By converting ever-more of life into supervised games.

In a contrived context of make-believe (but *only* in that context) it is possible both to be an indulged victim and at the same time *act* like one of the teachers.

What matters most – PC or societal function?

Originally, the PC elite covertly recognized that since these supervised games (education, public administration, law, the arts, mainstream religion) are merely make-believe optional extras, the *real business of life* must go on elsewhere.

So that the police, the military, the economy, science and technology all (until recently) remained broadly meritocratic – at most the victim groups would be used as window dressing, puppets or mouthpieces.

*

Well that was *then*…

However, since the PC elite do not believe in reality, therefore they do not believe in truth, so they lie all the time (because it is expedient): lie to themselves, and lie to each other, as well as to outsiders.

So of course *by now* they have long since lost sight of what they originally knew: that the system can *only* carry on *if* make-believe supervised games are not allowed to interfere with the serious stuff – the vital, frontline social functions: the police, the military, the economy, and science and technology.

The logic of PC is fatal to the preconditions of PC.

*

Nowadays, the PC elite have entered the realms of delusional psychosis – inside their thought prison they just *assume* that the important stuff will happen *automatically* and without attention or need for tough long-term choices; indeed will not just 'happen' but grow forever *despite* the imposition of PC priorities and their enforcement as being more important than primary social functions.

*

Excuses are not tolerated for PC failures, while failures of primary function are softened, hidden and 'magiced-away' with public relations spin: the military might be excused losing wars, the police might fail to prevent serious crime or fail to control riots, terrorists may slay at will, unemployment and inflation might both rise, science and technological breakthroughs might dry-up – but none of this is real, none of it *matters* so long as all social institutions become ever-more PC: more 'diverse', more 'environmentally-friendly' and so on.

*

Science and technology will, it is assumed, continue to provide breakthroughs; the economy will continue to expand by increased productivity; the police will maintain public order – indeed (since people will have PC attitudes) there will be less need for police; the military will keep us safe – indeed (since PC will make us better people) we will not have so many enemies…

*

Individuals and institutions will be forgiven pathetic ineffectiveness, gross inefficiency, neglect, incompetence, dishonesty, violence, corruption, fraud, abuse… forgiven absolutely anything *except* transgressions of the primary PC taboos.

*

For political correctness the *necessary* stuff just happens, naturally, spontaneously.

But the *important* stuff is done to us, done *for* us, by the elite PC supervisors.

Political correctness is now the primary reality, a thought prison into which *everything without exception* must be fitted.

Virtue in political correctness = altruism, un-selfishness

Political correctness is a secular ideology based on moral principle. It has its own conception of virtue.

From a secular perspective, the highest virtue, and perhaps the *only* virtue, is *altruism*: helping others at cost to oneself.

Other forms of human cooperation are disvalued – altruistic cooperation is regarded as the primary virtue.

*

Altruism is contrasted with the opposite vice of selfishness. Altruism is un-selfishness.

*

But, ideally, altruism must be pure – which means an altruism untainted by any *possibility* of selfishness, which means altruism untainted by any degree of personal advantage (untainted, therefore, even by perceptual pleasure).

PC morality is essentially altruism; and the highest altruism is disinterested.

*

(From an other-worldly religious perspective altruism is a subordinate virtue – there are other more important things than helping others in a material sense. But from a secular perspective, unselfish altruism is primary and frames almost the whole of moral discourse. PC altruism can therefore be seen a secular objectification of Christian 'charity'. While charity/ Agape is an individual, voluntary expression of The Good; by contrast secular PC altruism is a coercive, procedural transfer of 'goods'.)

*

Most, or all, forms of *naturally-occurring* altruism in biology are, in fact, conceptualized as merely indirect forms of self-interest. For example: altruism towards relatives promotes one's own genes; altruism towards allies brings cooperative benefits (you scratch my back then I'll scratch yours).

Some instances of apparent biological altruism are merely selfish long-termism (or "enlightened self-interest"), while others are *genetic* self interest coming into conflict with the interests of a specific organism (when an individual honey bee sacrifices her life to make more likely the survival of her extended family in the hive).

Even the altruism of Christianity is conceptualized by political correctness as being tainted and corrupted by the desire for heavenly happiness: so (from a PC perspective) Christians are 'merely', (albeit – it is assumed – delusionally) selfishly sacrificing themselves in this world in order to gain more happiness in the next.

(In fact, a Christian life is better understood as transformative – a change in *perspective* from worldly to heavenly, a moving-towards communion with God. But, of course, to political correctness all that kind of thing is just nonsense – either mad or manipulative nonsense.)

*

Altruism marks an important cleavage point between Leftist PC and Right wing secular conservatism, libertarianism and reaction. For the secular Right, the reality that altruism is tainted with selfishness is accepted – indeed it is embraced as a means to the end of greater functional effectiveness.

For the secular Right, selfishness is not exactly *good*, but is regarded as potentially *leading to good* under a competitive system of natural selection such as market economics.

But this attitude strikes the Left as merely amounting to a complacent or cruel acceptance of suffering, indeed an attitude of 'Greed is Good': promoting human selfishness; hence the worst conceivable wickedness for PC.

*

Political correctness recognizes that the secular Right has no conception of 'original sin' and regards human beings as intrinsically but blamelessly selfish, e.g. because evolved from selfish ancestors.

The secular Right accepts that kin selection means that humans tend to favour their families; that people with common interests will spontaneously make alliances for their own strategic benefit; that individuals will always be prone to corruption by selfishness, hedonism and short-termism – and the secular Right simply *tolerates* these problems so long as things, on the whole, are working well; or when eradicating a specific abuse seems likely to cause more functional problems than it solves.

Unprincipled materialistic pragmatism is therefore basic to the secular political Right – i.e. the tendency to accept and work-with human sin – and this is precisely why Leftists, including the PC, feel morally-superior to conservatives and libertarians.

Disinterested altruism and moral superiority

Disinterested altruism is the reason why the politically correct Left feel themselves to be virtuous, feel themselves morally superior to the Right; feel, indeed, *morally superior to all previous forms of human morality including all religions*: because the PC ideal is to be aiming at the unselfish material (hence measurable) good of others *without any material personal reward whatsoever.*

*

Naturally the individual PC person always will, indeed always *must*, fail to attain this ideal; naturally individual humans *always* fail to be impersonally altruistic. They can't help it!

But this merely emphasizes that individual selfishness is 'original sin' for the PC – and the implication is that *as an ideal* individuals ought to be, and need to be, subordinated to *impersonal mechanisms for coercively implementing altruism at the social level* – regardless of the consequences.

*

In fact, PC is a 'logical' (albeit erroneous) response to the ultimate problem of altruism regarded as the primary moral value; the psychological paradox that if being altruistic makes you happy, then you are being rewarded, therefore you are not really being altruistic but merely self-indulgent.

If you help others because you *enjoy* helping others then your altruism is not pure. But for PC, others ought to be treated altruistically whatever your feelings on the matter may happen to be.

*

To be 'pure', altruism therefore *should not make you happy*, should leave you unmoved at least, and preferably should make you miserable (but you do it anyway).

Only if altruism *makes you suffer* can you be sure that you are not merely doing it for your own selfish motives.

But if altruism makes people suffer, they will not voluntarily do it!

Therefore, true altruism *ought to be* coercive.

For PC, coercive altruism is a higher morality than voluntary charity precisely *because* it yields no personal gratification. Indeed, underlying PC is the notion that charitable people do not *deserve* the feelings of satisfaction associated with charitable giving, since they had no right in the first place to possession of the goods which they are allocating.

*

(Coercive altruism is also seen by PC as intrinsically more *dependable* as a basis for provision of goods, since voluntary charity can be withdrawn. Suppose people stop enjoying helping others, or come to believe that particular 'others' do not deserve so much 'help' – what then? Better make the process mandatory and procedural… In reality, voluntary charity is usually more effective and coercive altruism may *not* be more dependable – but for PC the facts are irrelevant: the superiority of coercive altruism is moral and intrinsic, therefore isn't a matter for empirical evaluation.)

*

The answer is that – as an individual – you should *be made to be altruistic*, and should be made miserable by your imposed altruism, and that this situation is abstractly good because then your own motivations will have nothing to do with your behaviour.

This, then, is an altruism which does not rely on the purity of human motivations.

Altruism *in spite of* 'original sin'.

*

Your job, in a system of PC, is therefore to *resign yourself* to your suffering – not to enjoy it, but not to complain about it either: simply to submit to it.

Willing but unhappy submission to coercive altruism is therefore the key concept.

For the idealistic PC individual, the ultimate ethical act is willingly to submit to being forced to be altruistic – not because you enjoy the process, but because you believe that submission to altruism is the highest value in an ultimate and abstract sense.

*

(The best possible job for a PC individual is therefore to work for a coercive bureaucracy that does altruistic good – *to hate your job* – and to do it anyway! As PC is itself an abstract system at its purest level; the satisfactions of PC are, naturally, themselves equally abstract.)

The insanity of pure abstract altruism

Pure disinterested altruism, imposed on all by abstract systems, is therefore a logical consequence of the moral primacy of pure altruism…

It is also insane and nihilistic.

PC is good *by definition* and for no other reason; especially not because PC has been *found to be* good.

After all, when there is no real reality, from what possible *authority* could derive the principle of the primacy of altruism?

*

What is more, PC is a creation of that minority of humans capable of abstract thought and who regard abstraction as primary, and experience as derived from theory. This perspective is coercively enforced on that majority of other humans who privilege experience above abstraction (e.g. the majority who spontaneously privilege natural law above moral inversion, beauty above shock, truth above subversion and so on…)

The mass majority therefore experience coercive altruism as merely alienating – either as aggressive or patronizing depending on whether they are at that moment givers or receivers.

Thought Prison

*

PC stands or falls by the fact of a secular intellectual ruling elite, and can be imposed widely by this elite *only* by the recent technologies of modern mass media.

And PC is only possible in a fully materialist and secular society: where this-worldly 'goods' and their just (i.e. altruistic) allocation can assume *ultimate* importance, over-riding all other considerations (such as the saving of souls).

*

It is this idealistic quest for pure impersonal abstract altruism, in a secular context, which has caused the anti-human, alienating, aggressive, patronizing, self-hating thought prison that is political correctness.

Immune to evidence

It is vital to understand that political correctness is immune to evidence – and I do not mean resistant to evidence, nor do I mean blindly dogmatic such that PC requires an overwhelming weight of evidence to be convinced; but I mean *utterly and completely immune to evidence* such that unanimity of incontrovertible evidence against PC is still insufficient to induce significant re-evaluation.

This is important to realize; since it makes clear that time, energy and personal resources expended on trying to convince PC advocates with evidence is just so much time and energy down-the-drain and lost - precious resources that could potentially have been expended constructively elsewhere.

*

The reason that PC is absolutely evidence-proof is that it operates at a wholly abstract level.

But the reason that it superficially appears that PC might potentially be open to evidential refutation is that, although abstract, PC is concerned exclusively with material proxy-measures of its abstractions.

That is the distinctive move which sets-apart PC from any preceding ideology.

*

Political correctness operates on the assumption that an abstract system of allocation is intrinsically superior to the lack of such a system; and the details can be worked-out in the fullness of time.

The reason why politically correct people believe in objective moral progress is that moral progress is equated with systematic altruism.

It is not so much that PC individuals believe *themselves* to be, personally morally superior to everybody who ever existed in past human generations (although in practice they often do); but that past generations lacked abstract mechanisms for altruistic allocation of goods and they were therefore *intrinsically* inferior.

For the sincerely PC; a world containing the United Nations, the European Union and Affirmative Action programs is *intrinsically* superior to any and all previous human societies which lacked such institutions.

My point is not that abstract systematic altruism is a means to some kind of end, but is an end in itself.

This is why *effectiveness* is of no interest, outcomes are of no concern and evidence has no relevance.

Indifference to outcomes

Political correctness is utterly indifferent to what happens to human beings – and I do not mean relatively insensitive to the consequences of its policies, but utterly indifferent.

Nothing which actually happens can ever challenge the ultimate virtue of political correctness.

Because PC regards *systems* as moral; not choices nor outcomes.

(Choice exists only to be manipulated or compelled, outcomes are of interest merely to provide stimulus to introduce abstract allocative systems.)

*

After all, PC policies are *always* introduced in the teeth of common sense and without any coherent reason to believe they would lead to good outcomes - why then should evidence accumulated after their implementation in any way affect their continuation?

My point is that political correctness has now reached such a level of abstraction that no evidence could ever challenge it.

Reform is impossible, on principle.

Thought Prison

This means that those who oppose political correctness should not (need not) waste time and energy on rational argument with people who are *truly* PC.

There is no way into or out-from the thought prison of sincere PC; no possibility of 'reform' or of modifying or moderating its basic nature.

Political correctness can only be accepted or ignored; obeyed or replaced.

Takeover by the PC elite – ten summary points

1. *Abstraction*. Many (not all) people of high intelligence have a preference or tendency to think abstractly rather than 'instinctively'.

Note: Abstraction is productive of nihilism: i.e. to the belief that there is no ultimate reality. If abstraction is regarded as providing the deepest access to reality, and since the power of abstraction depends on the vicissitudes of human mental functioning, then to the abstracting mind all is intangible, changeable, disconnected from spontaneity, from common sense, from emotional-underpinning. To the compulsively abstracting intellectual, reality tends to be perceived as dependant on the thinking mind – *a solipsistic play of shadows*, momentary distractions, meaningless sufferings and equally meaningless pleasures. Abstraction is indeed very useful in some situations in some societies – but it is like a mental pathology in other circumstances. Indeed, it is probably best to regard a strong disposition to abstraction as primarily a mental pathology; but one which has some useful specific functions (e.g. mathematics, science, invention) in certain types of society.

*

2. *Secularization*. Loss of belief in the ultimate nature of reality as transcendent, immaterial and other-worldly. A focus on this-world:

specifically (i) the measurable and (ii) the subjective (which two are fused: the subjective rendered measurable by proxy).

*

3. *Abstract Materialism.* The combination of abstraction and secularization therefore leads to an elite world view which is materialistic (this-worldly) and which explains things in terms of abstract forces and dispositions.

*

4. *Spirituality of materialism.* The purest, most idealistic morality from this perspective is therefore an abstract but non-transcendent spirituality of the material.

Note: A clear early example is Marxism, which is all about economics – about the production and distribution of material goods. Yet at the same time, material production and distribution is explained abstractly, and linked with a spirituality. The end result is that in Marxism the matter of the production and distribution of material goods becomes the highest level of human *moral* concern. Marxism was the first large scale morality of altruism – in which altruism was made abstract and involuntary (in replacement for the earlier personal and voluntary 'noblesse oblige', charitable alms-giving and philanthropy). So, Marxism therefore removed virtue from the individual and from the realm of choice, and made morality a socially-imposed abstract process. Under pure Marxism there were no good individuals, only the good society.

*

5. *Psychological 'goods'.* Political correctness extends a concern with the production and distribution of material goods to include the production and allocation of *psychological* goods. So that PC is

concerned by such matters as happiness, suffering, respect and self-respect: mostly *status*.

*

6. *Operational definitions.* However, since PC is materialist, intangible psychological factors require *operational definition* in terms of material proxy measures: so that happiness/ suffering may be equated with income and wealth, or with the results of surveys such as happiness ratings or crime levels, or with measures of health; status is operationally equated with occupancy of certain jobs, or attendance at specific educational establishments, or possession of educational certificates, and so on.

Therefore the abstract spirituality of materialism is underpinned by concrete operational measures of a material nature; such that the monitoring, prediction and manipulation of these material measures is equated with the (intangible) psychological states with which they are taken to be causally-correlated.

Note: Following the pattern of Marxism, in political correctness there are no good individuals, and no good individual choices or decision; but in contrast with Marxism neither is there a 'good society' – since only impersonal and mandatory procedures or mechanisms of allocation can be morally good. Immoral individuals are defined as such due to their necessarily-selfish defiance of impartial allocative procedure. Such reactionaries are guilty not for what they actually do, nor for the actual consequences of their actions, but for their defiance of objective and involuntary process.

*

7. *Intellectual meritocracy.* All societies are meritocratic to a degree – although the nature of the merit varies (for instance merit may be military prowess for a man, beauty for a woman) and the

rapidity of meritocratic sorting (i.e. social mobility) varies – sometimes a few years, sometimes a few generations. Throughout the twentieth century 'merit' became equated with intellectual ability and attainment – and a society developed in which the intellectual elite were the ruling class.

Almost all the main social functions therefore became dominated by intellectually selected personnel; but especially public administration, education and the mass media – the means of public discourse and communication.

Intellectual meritocracy promoted the most compulsively abstracting people, and allowed the pathology of abstraction to operate un-checked at the highest levels of social organization; the tendency expanding and evolving without effective feedback from common sense and spontaneity.

8. *Bureaucracy.* Also throughout the twentieth century, there was a massive expansion in the bureaucracy – the employment of almost all intellectuals within bureaucracies, and the linkage of all bureaucracies with public administration. So the modern society became interconnected by a bureaucratic web of laws, regulations, subsidies and coercive sanctions. And these bureaucracies became less personal – with all major decisions being taken by committee, and by vote.

*

9. *Mass media growth.* The mass media (staffed increasingly by intellectuals) grew to occupy ever more of the time and attention of the population.

*

10. *PC dominant.* So by the late twentieth century the massively interconnected bureaucracy and mass media meant that – for the

68

first time – the abstracting intellectual meritocratic elite could impose their distinctive morality on the rest of the population; and political correctness was established.

A positive feedback loop was established, by which the increasingly abstract and increasingly monopolistic 'PC reality' – created by the intellectual elite – continuously fed the abstract secular psychology of that same intellectual elite; such that the elite both made and experienced only that which was politically correct. Thus the circuit was closed.

Cut-off from normal human psychology, common sense and contradictory evidence; the hermetically-sealed system of PC expanded rapidly from the mid-1960s: the intellectual elite amplifying the influence of PC; PC amplifying the influence of the intellectual elite.

Not fundamentally egalitarian, after all

The relationship of political correctness to the egalitarian impulse, the desire for equality, is interesting. So much of PC rhetoric concerns equality that it superficially seems as if equality of distribution of goods is the goal of political correctness.

Yet this cannot be correct, since in practice PC imposes group preferences and inverts (but does not abolish) inequality.

*

It seems that even a situation of near monopoly allocation of 'goods' is compatible with a system of PC, indeed celebrated by PC – so long as the monopoly is of a favoured group.

*

Equality is not, therefore, the deepest impulse for political correctness.

What is deepest in political correctness is moral opposition to – and the desire therefore to subvert and invert – the existing or historical state of affairs brought about by individual agency and spontaneous or 'natural' causes.

Whatever state of affairs existed in the past or currently exists *in the absence of an abstract system of allocation* is regarded by PC as *intrinsically unjust on principle*, and without need for evidence of actual injustice.

*

So, actual, real world equality of outcome is a matter of near indifference to political correctness; except as 'evidence' of the need for PC systems of coercive allocation.

Political correctness merely *uses* egalitarianism instrumentally as a way of generating policies. But egalitarianism is not really necessary – because policies are primarily oppositional, subversive or inversional.

*

In other words, PC looks at the human social world *as it is and has been*, that is to say a world of multiple causal processes and without any overall master system of allocation, and regards this situation as necessarily unjust – ultimately because of intrinsic human selfishness ('original sin'): human selfishness will always affect human choice, choice will always therefore lead to injustice, and therefore injustice will exist so long as human choice is allowed.

Equality is not necessary to political correctness, but in-equality has the advantage of being amenable to definitions, measurement, monitoring – and being made the basis of bureaucratic procedure.

*

But indeed *any* argument is suitable as a basis for PC to attack *any* existing state of affairs which relies on individual choice, free will.

The dissatisfaction (actual, inferred or imputed) of just a single symbolic person or one obscure victim group is enough to trigger

71

wholesale change – just so long as this dissatisfaction can somehow be linked to the introduction of a system of coercive, abstract, altruistic allocation.

The definition of happiness under PC

For political correctness, happiness is not an empirical *consequence* of PC policies.

Rather, happiness is the moral duty of individuals living under PC; happiness is the state of virtuous humans when PC allocative policies are operating.

*

Ultimately, for political correctness happiness is abstract, not perceptual.

Indeed, given that PC is totalitarian and coercive, this is necessarily the case: people are happy under a system of political correctness precisely because the system tells them they are happy, and expressions of misery are not tolerated.

*

To believe that one *is* happy, yet not actually to *feel* happy – that is to be *abstractly* happy!

The Principle of Inversion

The big problem for PC – in a system where human agency is regarded as intrinsically wicked – is to determine (or somehow just decide) what distribution of goods counts as altruistic?

Clearly this question has no ultimate answer, since PC denies the validity of both reason and experience (as well as the possibility of divine revelation); instead there are a series of pragmatic answers to what counts as altruistic.

*

The *principle of subversion and inversion of whatever is individual, spontaneous and natural* therefore serves as a 'rule-of-thumb' to identify problems and to generate aims for the solutions.

However these aims are inexplicit, because so obviously absurd. Hence the need for camouflage with false but asserted goals of such as being more egalitarian, humanitarian, compassionate, efficient… anything will suffice.

*

How does inversion operate? Simple:

If *men* spontaneously tend to become leaders, then an allocative system should favour women; if humans are naturally *hetero*sexual, then allocative systems should favour any preference *except* heterosexuality; if a particular group rules and another is ruled, then the allocative system should invert the existing hierarchy.

*

Being merely subversive and crudely inversional, the positive policies of political correctness are therefore arbitrary, changeable over time – generating a stream of stimulating novelties for the jaded bureaucratic palate.

Often PC policies will make things worse from any common-sensical or experiential perspective. But none of that matters, since the politically correct solution is always *intrinsically* superior in so far as it removes the scope or possibility of individual selfishness.

The solution to any (undeniable) problems caused by PC is always more of the same: residual problems are framed as insufficient PC.

(Or covert resistance to PC from reactionaries!)

*

Always, always, everywhere: PC aims at the removal of individual freedom and choice; the reversal of whatever is spontaneous, natural or historic; the inversion of what *is*.

PC Utopia

The pure and idealistic politically correct elite intellectual aspires (as his highest goal in life) to create a perfect and autonomous mechanism for *devising* altruistic principles then coercively *implementing them* on all humans.

Having created this mechanism for the definition and imposition of abstract altruism, his own fate is a matter of indifference...the PC elite intellectual might step-back and watch, might be rewarded, or might be destroyed – but the allocation machine, once built, will just keep running: just keep-on compelling wicked individual humans to do that which is abstractly just.

*

A living-death – a thought prison for all of society, a prison in which the ultimate PC human wickedness (i.e. selfishness) is impossible because every single human decision related to the allocation of the goods of life has been subordinated to a system of abstract altruism – *this* is the covert Utopian dream of the politically correct.

Atomic individuals, atomic acts

In trying to get to the bottom of political correctness, it is necessary to discard as inessential some of its most prominent features.

One of these prominent features of PC that is not really fundamental are 'group preferences': those 'affirmative action' policies that identify a favoured group and award them preferential treatment (under the rationale of 'social justice').

This is perhaps the most obvious, and destructive, aspect of PC – yet it is merely a transitional stage. If PC became more powerful, and succeeded in imposing mandatory abstract altruistic systems on acts of allocation of goods – then group preferences would swiftly be abolished.

In PC Utopia, all groups would be dissolved, all humans would be treated as atomic *individuals*.

Indeed, the process would not stop there: each allocation of goods (each decision or choice that had any affect on the distribution of valued human outcomes) would be treated as an atomic act, and brought under abstract rules.

So, PC is not only destructive of groups, but eventually of individuals.

Hence the totalitarianism of political correctness.

All groups seen as interest groups

Although political correctness *uses* groups, it does not believe in the *reality* of groups.

*

Specifically, PC acts on the basis that all human groups are merely 'interest groups'; that is contingent, tactical and temporary alliances, held together only by cooperation in pursuit of selfish material gains.

This can be seen by what are sometimes seen as apparent paradoxes or slip-ups in the application of PC policies, but which in reality reveal what PC truly cares about and what it is merely using tactically.

*

One significant illustration is that PC focuses on the moral importance of group preferences or affirmative action – yet makes little effort precisely to define group membership. Indeed, quite the opposite – group membership is continually being blurred and expanded.

If PC was serious about group preferences, then PC would define group membership very sharply so as to exclude undeserving people from the preferences. Yet in fact group membership is typically a matter of *self-definition*, and there are seldom any attempts to challenge self-definitions with evidence.

Indeed, proof that someone has made a false claim of group membership in order to obtain privileges and preferences is often ignored – or the liar is actually supported emotionally: presumably because such lies reinforce the fictions of PC.

Group membership is then more-or-less a matter of chosen lifestyle; for someone electively to adopt the lifestyle of a PC-favoured group is, in practice, supportive of political correctness – and whether or not they are *entitled* to membership is of subordinate importance.

*

At a deep level, then, group identities allocated by political correctness are arbitrary to the extent that they are of peripheral concern to the system.

PC merely *uses* groups in the game of power politics to attack, subvert and force-into-submission that which it opposes: which is the historic, spontaneous state-of-affairs resulting from individual choice and moral autonomy.

*

The priority, as always, is coercively to impose on society a mandatory abstract system for allocating goods – abstract systems are *always* preferable to human agency, because agency will *certainly* become corrupt, while abstract system has the *potential* to be perfected.

Groups are merely a weapon in this fight.

PC-favoured groups are assumed to be weak and controllable

At present, human agency is attacked by generating various *gangs* (interest groups) under various banners of egalitarianism, anti-racism, anti-sexism and all the rest.

These gangs are made, are created, by PC *patronage* – by group preferences (group-based propaganda, laws, regulations, subsidies, exemptions etc).

The gangs function as anti-agency tactical shock troops: to be thrown against autonomous choice wherever it is identified.

But because these groups have been created by PC patronage, they are neither feared nor regarded as potential rulers. For PC the anti-agency gangs are merely useful but temporary mobs.

The assumption is that these mobs will disassemble and dissolve into their component parts as soon as the conduit of PC, patronage is switched-off.

*

Political correctness is *not* therefore trying to install favoured groups into *power*, and does not *fear* such groups becoming powerful, because PC regards them simply as 'creatures' of PC.

Because the dominance of PC patronage gangs is unspontaneous, unnatural, unhistorical; their status is wholly artificial, and utterly *parasitic* on PC for their existence and survival.

In other words, by inversion of natural, spontaneous order; political correctness ensures that favoured groups are unstable, weak and dependent.

That which PC has created: PC can control.

*

At root PC is therefore not trying to favour certain groups as a matter of strategy; rather PC is tactically using one group against another group, with the strategic intent of weakening and eventually destroying *all* human groups.

PC not fundamentally 'multicultural'

Political correctness has become almost synonymous with favouring 'multiculturalism' or 'diversity' – yet this is not a *core* value of PC; and is indeed one of those tactical beliefs which PC adopts only as a means to an end.

In PC Utopia there would be no multiculturalism – indeed there would be no 'culture' at all.

*

In other words, while political correctness does indeed 'hate' Western Culture, this hatred is only a by-product of the fact that PC hates culture as such (since culture is an unplanned outcome of innumerable individual choices, and PC regards all individuals as irredeemably selfish and inevitably corrupt).

*

The PC hatred of Western Culture is merely a matter of using the excuse of promoting 'other' cultures as a method of destroying culture *per se*.

As soon as the dominant culture is destroyed and another culture has been artificially created and inserted to replace it, PC can then turn to destroying those other cultures.

Patronage of the new hegemony would be withdrawn, and those cultures which PC created and sustained will collapse, then 'culture' will itself be displaced by abstract systems to which individual choice would be subordinated.

*

In PC Utopia there is no 'need' for culture!

People would behave properly *because they had no choice.*

Good people would be happy about this; bad people would, presumably, be miserable – but they would be made to 'do the right thing' anyway.

Orthodox religion is immune to PC incentives

Political correctness subverts existing social arrangements and replaces them with groups who owe their existence to PC; and does this by manipulation using material incentives: bribes, subsidies and accolades on the one hand; vilification, fines and aggression on the other hand.

But there are some groups that are immune to material incentives: namely traditional, orthodox religions.

Secularism made PC possible, democracy made PC irresistible, intellectual meritocracy made PC happen, the mass media made PC pervasive – but orthodox religion will be the nemesis of PC.

*

Atheistic political correctness simply *cannot believe* that there are people in the world who are motivated by religion more than by material goods. In this PC is incurably blind: its discourse has neither the vocabulary nor the conceptual capability to include religion.

*

So, when there is a devout, other-worldly religion that is explicitly, actively, demonstrably hostile to the values of PC; and which cannot be subverted by material incentives nor by mainstream mass media; then this phenomenon simply *cannot* be taken seriously by PC.

Other-worldly orthodox religions will either be altogether unnoticed, or else religious behaviour is *explained-away* in falsely PC terms such as having a covert secular agenda, responding to material needs or expressing lifestyle preferences.

But (in some cases at least) orthodox religion really is buffered-against secularism, materialism and lifestyle.

Such religions encourage and enable people to disregard material incentives, to sacrifice this world for the next, to suffer and die for their beliefs.

*

Orthodox religion is indeed pre-modern: was not created by PC, is not sustained by PC, does not *need* PC; is indeed intrinsically and implacably opposed to PC – root and branch – and has survived vastly more opposition than PC ever would be able or willing to impose on it.

Therefore against devoutly orthodox religion PC is *powerless*.

(You cannot fight a foe who is advancing in the middle of your blind spot; you cannot repel a foe when your arrows bounce off the armour of faith.)

*

The only question is *which* religion will defeat PC in each specific place.

Something to think about…

PC as a Christian heresy

Since political correctness has Christian features and comes from Christian historical roots; does this then mean that PC is a Christian heresy? – in the sense that PC is the *fault* of Christianity, perhaps an inevitable outcome of Christianity?

Well… yes in a *way*; but actually *no*, not at all!

*

Political correctness is indeed post-Christian; but the proper emphasis is on the *post*, not on the Christian.

*

It is the fact that PC has *rejected* the *core* of Christianity which is of significance; not that PC *retains* some *peripheral*, distorted and fragmentary aspects of Christian ethics.

Specifically, it is the rejection of the *pre-requisites* of Christianity which cause the problem of PC.

Political correctness is fundamentally (not accidentally) hostile to Christianity, basically orientated-against Christianity.

That is, political correctness is hostile to 'orthodox' Christianity – Christianity as ideally conceptualized and practiced in most places and over most of the past 2000 years.

PC is not particularly hostile to the modern 'liberal Christianity' of mainstream Churches – a worldly Christianity which is liberal first and Christian only insofar as Christianity does not conflict with PC.

*

Underlying PC there is a nihilistic rejection of reality; and this nihilism was caused when orthodox Christianity was rejected; and nihilism was the means by which orthodox Christianity was rejected.

In order to get rid of Christianity, what was rejected was *a whole way of orientating humanity in reality*: most of it pagan, some of it monotheistic, a relatively small amount of it being specifically Christian.

So, PC Post-Christianity is not just Post-Christian, but also Post-Monotheist and Post-Pagan. None of these traditional religious perspectives make any kind of sense to PC.

*

Politically correct post-Christianity rejects (*inter alia*) the soul, the immaterial realm, life after death, the supernatural (e.g. angels and demons), the actuality of permanent objective reality, the possibility of knowledge of reality, the reality of the transcendental Good (and its components Truth, Beauty and Virtue), the possibility of God or gods, a personal relationship with the divine, the possibility of divine revelation, miracles, prophecy... and so on and on.

*

Being *'post'* all-this-stuff is the very *essence* of PC – and the aspirations of core political correctness have nothing *necessarily* to do with the fragmentary and distorted Christian elements currently residual in PC.

*

(Indeed, any totalitarian ideology such as political correctness – which implicitly aims at the destruction of all human agency – free will – is about as anti-Christian as it is possible to be. It would, if successfully implemented, make Christianity impossible, since belief could never be *chosen*.)

*

Put it like this: political correctness is always, purposefully, fundamentally and permanently anti-orthodox-Christian; and only sometimes, accidentally, superficially, fragmentarily and temporarily 'christian'.

Western civilization cannot be saved

It is a major goal of conservative politics to 'save' Western Civilization.

Yet this is not a coherent belief, nor is it possible, nor is it desirable.

*

The big problem with 'saving' the West is that it is precisely Western Civilization which created Leftism: Communism, Socialism, Liberalism, and Political Correctness; bureaucracy; committees; 'modern art'; 'human rights'; pacifism...

It is Western Civilization which is destroying *itself*.

*

The self-destroying aspects of the West have always been there, and they permeate or are woven-into the whole.

Western Civilization has always been changing – not merely superficially, but deeply. It has never been stable – not even for two generations in a row.

There is no evidence that The West ever *could* be stable – and everything suggests the opposite.

The West is perpetually in transition: it has no essence: it is evolutionary.

*

There is much to suggest that the political Left is indeed *the main line* of a Western Civilization which was pre-programmed to self-destruction.

Meanwhile the political Right has been merely applying intermittent braking on this suicidal journey; imposing temporary corrections which sustain the West in the short term   but only at the cost of entrenching its long-term and underlying errors.

If so, the West cannot be saved. To 'save' the West would entail re-winding and recovering a pre-Western perspective then re-running the process – but hoping that *this time* the desired attributes would re-emerge *without* self-destructive Leftism.

But the West has self-destruction built-in; or rather Western civilization is built-*over* a simultaneously self-dug pit of nothingness into which it will, sooner or later, fall.

*

How can you save something which *so much* wants to kill itself?

Take your eye off Western Civilization for *just a moment* and it will be swinging from the rafters with its own belt around its neck.

The millennium-deep roots of political correctness

The West took a turn toward legalism, logic and bureaucracy around AD 1000 ('the Great Schism') when the Roman Catholic Church (gradually) broke away from the Eastern Orthodox Catholic Church centred in the Byzantine Roman Empire with its capital in Constantinople.

Like most long term policy mistakes, the East-West schism was initially richly rewarded (otherwise the mistake would not have been made) – since it led to tremendous 'progress' in first philosophy and scholarship (especially Thomas Aquinas) with the development of universities, then later in science and technology, and later still in the economy.

*

But schism led on to more schisms, with no end in sight.

The benefits and the mistake were alike in being built-on continuous specialization of function; progressive specialization of all functions, without limit.

The Great Schism built-into the thought systems of the West a fatal error, of which PC is a remote and indirect consequence.

*

Thought Prison

Once modernity (progressive specialization) has been built into a system, it *cannot stop itself* – and it cannot stop itself because continual specialization creates (or indeed itself *is*) continually increasing autonomy of parts.

The nature of the process is division and sub-division and sub-sub-division and so on; and it becomes ever-more-impossible to harmonize the parts until the whole loses coherence.

You just get more and more specialization of function until the whole social system falls apart into useless fragments; and all the King's Horses and all the King's men cannot put Humpty together again.

By secularizing knowledge, by creating The University – (by making philosophy autonomous of the Church instead of having learning institutionally focused in monasteries) the West *eventually* made political correctness – which is now *everywhere and inescapable.*

And PC is the West's Nemesis, because the West cannot decisively overturn PC without overturning that which made it The West.

With PC the West has gotten what it wanted, what it asked-for; has gotten exactly what it *deserves.*

*

So, the West cannot overcome PC without ceasing to be The West.

Yet, if this overturning of PC does not happen, then the West will itself be subverted by PC.

In other words, The West is built upon error: its strength is also its weakness; its power is also that which is self-destroying; even as

The West built its great structures it was simultaneously gnawing at their foundations.

*

Here is the double-bind:

To be *anti-PC* is to be anti-The West (always in tendency, albeit not by intention)

At the same time, to be *pro-PC* is also to be anti-The West (always in tendency, and also by intention)

And/ So/ But The West never was sustainable.

*

Just so soon as The West began to implement its assumptions towards completion (which is political correctness), just so soon The West began purposefully (as well as accidentally) to destroy itself.

Could resurgent nationalism save Western civilization from PC?

After secularization eroded religious cohesion in modernizing societies (from the 1700s), there was an era of secular nationalism in developed countries.

And some opponents of PC see resurgent secular nationalism as an antidote to the cultural decline caused by political correctness.

Accepting that political correctness is cultural suicide, and leaving aside the question of whether or not it would be beneficial, is it *likely* that resurgent secular nationalism can unify the Right and could reverse the cultural suicide of PC?

*

Nationalism is indeed a powerful unifier and motivator – perhaps *the* most powerful form of *secular* cohesion; because nationalism has potential to bring together all classes, both sexes, young and old, sometimes even several ethnicities and religions.

*

But a secular nationalism would nowadays have a strongly different character from most secular nationalisms of the past.

A modern nationalism might perhaps save the nation as a political unit – but it would not save the national *culture*.

Furthermore, secular nationalisms of the past seem to have had little staying power – fading within only two or three generations.

So nationalism would be – at best – a sticking-plaster, a band-aid.

But is it even that?

*

When secular nationalism was an effective political force (e.g. from the 19th up to mid-20th centuries in the West), it was a movement which grew spontaneously, it did not need much encouragement.

Furthermore, in most countries – perhaps all of them – nationalism *originated with the intellectual elites* – typically the lower ranks of the elites (i.e. the most numerous ranks of the ruling class): people like school teachers and lower-level administrators, also journalists and artists.

This even applies to Germany – nationalism had been going for more than a century among the elites, the *Dichter und Denker* – poets and thinkers – before it was rather suddenly hijacked by the mostly lower class National Socialists reacting against International Communism.

Past nationalism was (often) primarily cultural and only secondarily about the national unit. When nationalism was expansive, one reason was that it aimed to include all instances of its national culture, ignoring the boundaries of existing political units (which it regarded as arbitrary and unjust).

*

In other words, past successful nationalisms were cultural and led by a cultural elite: nationalism was a political movement of 'clerks' and therefore, even before it got-going, old-style nationalists *already controlled the media and mass communications.*

*

Past successful nationalisms therefore originated with exactly those groups which are nowadays *the most politically correct*, least nationalistic, most in favour of multi-culturalism.

Modern nationalists are precisely *excluded* from the mass media.

Any modern nationalism would therefore need to be very different from past nationalisms.

*

Of course new things can happen – and we are, after all, in an unprecedented situation: i.e. the new experience of deliberate, strategic, sustained, cultural and genetic suicide by the intellectual elites, taking their nations with them.

Perhaps such a novel situation will inevitably lead to unforseen types of political response? – perhaps including a nationalism which is *opposed* by the exact groups which (in previous nationalisms) supported it?

In line with this, what does seem to be resurgent in the West (to some extent – maybe limited) is a lower class, populist nationalism.

What we are seeing is a nationalism led by the skilled working class rather than the teachers, lower civil servants and writers – we are seeing a nationalism of tradesman rather than clerks.

However, to be successful against PC (when PC is sustained by an intellectual ruling class and the mass media), such a nationalism of the tradesmen would (surely?) need both to be anti-intellectual and to impose tight control over the mass media.

A resurgent secular nationalism would therefore seek to replace the effete, irrelevant, decadent clerks with sensible skilled workers.

And since a new nationalism of tradesman lacks access to the media and mass communications (and also lacks the skill to use them), it would be implacably opposed by the media and mass communications systems; anti-PC resurgent secular nationalism would therefore naturally be *anti* the media and mass communications, as well as anti their personnel.

*

A nationalism of the upper working class/ lower middle class would necessarily promote a radically simplified, popular and accessible *folk* culture, suitable for those who are only secondarily concerned with culture as a leisure-time activity, or as a means to other ends.

Tradesman class leaders are likely to regard *high* culture with hostility, based on the suspicion (often accurate; although – importantly – not entirely so) that high culture is a tool for forcing the tradesmen class into subordinate status and for elevating the status of the clerks.

*

In such a society, 'warrior virtues' would presumably predominate - courage, decisiveness, loyalty, perhaps common-sense and concrete effectiveness; and there would consequently be only relatively few high status, ruling positions for intellectuals, high-artists and abstract thinkers.

In a tradesman-led nationalism, intellectuals would, rather, be allocated subordinate status as functionaries.

*

(Recall that historically – and still in most of the world – aside from relatively few senior 'priests'; the bulk of intellectuals were of modest and circumscribed status; such as secretaries and notaries, teachers, servants, slaves, outcasts, itinerants, eunuchs and celibates.)

Characteristics of a new secular nationalism

Since the modern elite or 'officer class' is truly, madly, deeply politically correct; *if* a nationalism were to arise (which seems unlikely) it would need to originate from and be led by the tradesman class – or, to put it another way, the Non-Commissioned Officer (NCO) class: that is to say a nationalism led by the Sergeants and Corporals; and not by the Majors and Captains.

*

All else being equal, under normal circumstances, an army led by Officers will be much more effective than an army led by NCOs.

But, it could be argued, these are not normal circumstances.

*

The modern situation in the West resembles that of a city under siege.

The city is threatened by an expanding parasite class ('sturdy beggars', or the 'undeserving poor' as GB Shaw termed them), by riots within and by the enemy without.

However, the Officers have become decadent.

The Officers find-uncouth, are-bored-by, scared-of, and have indeed come to *loathe* the NCOs and squaddies of their own city.

(*Noblesse oblige* is a thing of the past, and socialism has long-since rejected its working class roots in favour of a 'rainbow coalition' of parasitic, underclass and designated-victim groups.)

*

Periodically, groups of indigents approach the besieged city gates.

Some are hopeless cases – displaced peasants from the surrounding area; some are shrewd merchants and traders from here and there – keen to work hard and make some money; some are petty criminals – others are not-so-petty criminals: gangsters and assorted thugs, thieves and beggars.

And some of the indigents at the gate are enemy fifth columnists – who intend at some point in the future to inflict violence and mayhem to aid the besiegers and take-over the city.

But whoever the indigents are, and whatever their intention, the Officers invariably feel sorry for them (sorrier than they do for their own NCOs and squaddies, or for the indigenes of the city); and so always let them *all* come through the gates and into the city (because to do otherwise would be to commit the ultimate and unforgiveable sin of *discrimination*); and direct the NCOs to make sure the new arrivals are *well taken care of* – by allocating them a generous share of the NCO and squaddies' rations and living quarters.

*

And within the cities own indigenous population are large mobs of sturdy vagrants who are either too feckless to be of any use, or

100

simply refuse to help with the defense of the walls (the parasitic sturdy beggars and underclass).

These muggers, robbers, beggars and barflys roam around fighting, having parties and looting. The NCOs are not exactly forbidden to intervene, but will be harshly punished if they transgress any of the very strict (and continually changing) rules of engagement. So the underclass are left alone to do their business.

On orders from the Officers, these sturdy vagrants receive a daily dole of bread and beer – also taken from the NCO and squaddies' supplies.

*

This situation of the Officers robbing the NCOs and squaddies to reward outsiders and vagrants is roughly (and in a purely materialist sense – which leaves-out the vital spiritual and religious dimension) the situation of the modern West.

*

Secular nationalism is (at minimum) an attempt to make effective the defense of the city – first to stop admitting, then to expel, outsiders, fifth columnists and parasites; and to suppress internal disorder.

But the Officers will not do this, and will indeed try to prevent it.

So, if the city has not fallen first (and that is a big 'if') then at some point, perhaps, there may be an NCO mutiny – and the army will be taken-over and run by the senior sergeants.

Because a city will be better defended by an army led by loyal NCOs, than by an army led by traitorous Officers.

If this kind of secular nationalism happens as a reaction against 'the treason of the clerks', then it would surely, *necessarily*, be accompanied by a powerful *anti-Officer* campaign – during which Officers would be purged from all significant positions of leadership – and replaced by Sergeants.

The outcome would be a pretty shambolic army, or society. Yet it would not have to be *well*-organized; only well-*enough*-organized to defeat the forces which oppose it.

If nothing else happens first, at some point in the cultural decline that is political correctness the point will be passed at which a nationalist NCO-led army will be more effective than an army led by anti-nationalist Officers.

*

Yet before this happens, it may well be that the city will fall to the enemy; and instead of being run by an NCO army of the indigenous population, the city will instead be taken-over by an Officer-led army of invaders.

Could a party of 'common sense' replace political correctness?

With the profound weakness of mainstream Christianity in the West (due to subversion by Leftism and subordination to PC), and with the weakness of old-style nationalism (led by the lower levels of the upper class – teachers, minor civil servants and journalists – who are now the most zealous of the politically correct), and with the unlikeliness of a new nationalism of the tradesman/ NCO class – then the most likely opposition to political correctness (especially in the USA) currently comes from populist, reactionary, secular groups based on *common sense*.

From a Christian perspective, such groupings are seriously sub-optimal – at best a temporary expedient. Nonetheless, supposing that common sense secularism was actually to become powerful – what then? Could it, would it provide a better alternative future than PC? What would that future be?

This can be predicted by considering the probable characteristics of such a grouping – and weighing-up the pros and cons.

*

Since so much of Western society is now corrupted by Leftism and implicated in PC, such a group would have to come from outside this – and in rejecting the psychotic delusionality of PC it would need to offer a common sense alternative which would be obvious

103

to plain, middling, productive people outwith the intelligentsia and their underclass of state-dependents.

And since a common sense party would be *reactive* against PC, we can infer its main features.

*

Here is a non-exhaustive list (in no particular order) of characteristics of a possible Common Sense (CS) party contrasted with the politically correct (PC) party.

CS ʋ PC

Natural and spontaneous versus Human designed

Reality is real and fixed versus Reality is relative and plastic

Coercive force versus Propaganda

Face to face versus Mass media

Concrete versus Abstract

Immediate versus Utopian

Instinctive versus Educated

Native versus Immigrant

Popular culture versus High art

Practical versus Theoretical

Invention versus Science

White versus Non-white

Heredity versus Culture

Apprenticeship versus Formal education

Thought Prison

Men versus Women

Recognition versus Certification

Selfish versus Altruistic

Personal authority versus Bureaucratic procedure

Heterosexual versus Homosexual

Heart versus Head

Gut versus Intellect

Local versus International

Tribal versus Outcast

Family versus Universalist

Real versus Ideal

Morality versus Law

Natural law versus Moral inversion

Courage versus Tolerance

Loyalty versus Subversion

Useful versus Useless

Duty versus Self-development

Productive versus Ideologically-sound

Money-grubbing versus Parasitic

Responsibilities versus Rights

Charity versus Needs

Hierarchy versus Egalitarianism

Genetic fertility versus Erotic sterility

*

This list suggests that *secular* modern politics boils down *either* to political correctness *or* what could be termed (and almost certainly would-be termed) a kind of 'fascism'.

In other words fascism is approximately what you get when political correctness is opposed with common sense.

Of course, the Left has been calling the Right fascist since the mid-1960s: I suggesting that in doing this *the Left are broadly correct*.

However, there are two important qualifications 1. that the fascist label properly applies only to the *secular* Right – not the religious Right; and 2. fascism is *not* synonymous with the Nazis – who were substantially a socialist and Leftist party, as the name of National Socialism implies.

Maybe at some point the secular Right will eventually stop fighting the 'fascist' label and become openly and explicitly fascist – but distancing themselves from the National Socialist type of (semi) fascism?

*

Thought Prison

The *religious* Right is not fascist: fascism is secular hence modern; and the religious Right is pre-modern and much more ancient than fascism. Indeed the religious Right was pretty much all there was in pre-modern times: conflict being between different varieties of religious Right.

The huge difference between religious Right and secular Right is that the religious Right seeks to rule society *primarily by religious principles*, by religious goals. By contrast the common sense secular Right ('fascism') is justified on the basis of this-worldly common sense goals: such as the aim to make its supporters happier and richer; to provide a glorious national or ethnic purpose; to forge a new community of the heart.

What is The Good?

The Good is the highest goal in life; but The Good as a unitary entity is hard to understand and to think about – and most people usually focus on three component transcendental Goods of Truth, Beauty and Virtue (moral good).

However, there is a problem in splitting up the Good – which is that people begin to evaluate the world using separate modalities of thought.

Truth becomes the province of first philosophy, then later science.

Beauty becomes the province of art.

*

And Virtue?

Virtue becomes religion – *the whole thing!*

Then later Virtue becomes a secular ideology.

Yes indeed, Virtue – or 'morality' – can become *the whole of a religion* – such that people cannot see that religion has anything to do with either Truth or Beauty.

*

Morality becomes the whole thing – the sole legitimate aim of human endeavor.

In which circumstance religion becomes legalistic, inevitably.

Virtue is then a matter of following a set of rules, of Laws.

Virtue is reduced merely to obedience.

*

But once religion is reduced to the pursuit of Virtue, and once Virtue is conceptualized in terms of Laws, and obedience to these Laws – then secular morality can dispense with religion.

So now we observe that 'morals' and 'ethics' seem to be autonomous from religion – forming an apparently independent realm of discourse; circular, mutually-reinforcing without foundation outside of persons – referenced solely to the subjective states of persons (as operationalized in public proxy measures).

And this free-floating, continually-changing secular morality is then turned-around and used to judge and evaluate the Virtuousness of those systems of religion from which it originated, which provided its original foundations – and secular morality finds religion deficient.

*

The pursuit of Virtue, detached from its unity with Truth and Beauty in the Good – is therefore a major pathology of Western thought.

Some Christian denominations – indeed *most of them*, are wholly-concerned with Virtue, and regard Truth and (especially) Beauty as of grossly subordinate importance.

*

The actual circumstances of this kind of religious life and practice may indeed be devoid of Beauty or hostile to Beauty.

Indeed, Beauty may be regarded as a *snare*, rather than a component of The Good.

And the same applies to mainstream secular ideologies – such as Communism, or modern liberal political correctness. These are *wholly Virtue orientated.*

Untruthfulness in pursuit of Virtue is not only tolerated but positively approved; destroying beauty and creating ugliness in pursuit of Virtue is similarly valued as evidence of moral seriousness.

Truthfulness is seen as pedantic and selfish; a passionate concern for beauty as trivial: a species of self-indulgent upper class Dandyism.

For the zealously politically correct, the most Virtuous *ought to be indifferent* to such matters as Truth and Beauty – noble minds should be wholly moral.

*

But lined-up against this partial pursuit of Virtue are similarly absurd, wicked and evil partial exaltations of Truth and Beauty – and these are also characteristic of modernity.

The partial pursuit of Truth leads to scientism; to the common and indeed dominating conviction that science, mathematics and the like are the *only valid forms of knowledge*; and that the true and dedicated scientist should pursue Truth indifferent to Virtue and Beauty – on the basis that the single-minded pursuit of Truth is intrinsically virtuous, and necessarily beautiful.

The equivalent situation in the arts can be seen when beauty becomes the exclusive province of specialized Art professionals, aesthetics becomes distinct from evaluations of Virtue and Truth – and the ideal is 'Art for Art's sake'.

*

So we reach, have *long-since* reached, a situation when the transcendental Goods have been split up and regarded as separable, regarded as amenable to separate pursuit; are indeed *contrasted* with each other and *pitted-against* each other by what are *de facto* interest groups such as priests, scientists and artists: each claiming the high ground, each trying to subordinate the others.

*

Yet The Good is in reality a unity: that which is Good is intrinsically and inevitably Virtuous, True and Beautiful.

Truth, Beauty and Virtue cannot *really* be separated.

*

The Good is not attained by being virtuous and then bolting-on truth and adding a layer of beauty; nor is it attained by a narrowly fanatical pursuit of precision and reliability then surrounding it with a halo of words that claim its ultimate virtuousness and an assertion of its special kind of beauty; nor by a belief that a novel, poem, painting, song – created to fulfill the criteria of these aesthetic forms – is intrinsically also an agent of the highest truth and tending to a special kind of human virtue...

For a Christian to aim at The Good is to regard it as characteristic of God; and to conceptualize the aim of life as the intention mystically to move-towards *communion* with God – to become more God-like.

The situation is that the True, Beautiful and Moral are merely aspects of the Good – and when they are not aspects of that unity then *they are not Good*.

The *discrete* pursuit of Truth, Beauty and Virtue as if they were distinct goals tends therefore to become subversive of the Good, may indeed become its opposite – have indeed already and long since become the opposite of Good.

*

For political correctness to act as if Virtue is higher than Truth and Beauty is therefore very swiftly to embrace *that which opposes The Good* – not merely the narrowly wicked (anti-virtuous) idea of Bad, but further to destroy the whole *capacity* for Good.

Political Correctness is purposefully subversive of The Good

PC is not ignorant of The Good – it knows what is The Good.

PC *must* indeed know enough about The Good, that it may subvert it.

And indeed, knowledge of The Good is built into humans: this is termed Natural Law.

*

The point of PC is that it systematically subverts Virtue, Beauty and Truth and pursues wickedness, ugliness and lies – and not by accident, not merely by ignorance nor by selfish short-termism – but as a matter of the highest principle.

*

In morality, PC pursues the-opposite-of-Virtue. It learns about spontaneous human morality – Natural Law – and it does... something else.

Political correctness subverts the natural and spontaneous. It reacts-against it. In practice it does the opposite, or what it conceives to be the opposite: PC inverts.

*

Where humans are motivated by love or duty, PC demands they be motivated by adherence to formal principles and procedures. Where humans spontaneously nurture and protect the family, PC attacks the family relentlessly and promotes any and all forms of social organization except the family. Because humans, like all animals, are heterosexual, PC promotes all other forms of sexuality. Because some humans are brave and heroic and those who are not tend to admire these traits; PC promotes careerism and expediency.

*

Because humans naturally love Beauty, and value those who create Beauty; therefore PC subverts Beauty and aggressively promotes dysphoric stimuli. Politically correct art is anti-Beauty – it regards The Beautiful as *Kitsch* at best and tyrannically fascist at worst; it is about creating expectations then thwarting them, it is about replacing harmony with dissonance, edification with shock, delight with horror, pleasing sounds with noise, elevating subjects with disgusting subjects, aesthetic elevation with visceral degradation.

*

And PC reacts against The Truth. Truth is to be subordinated to the goal of subversion. Unwanted Truths are Hate Facts. Universally known Truths are replaced with narrow scraps of bureaucratically defined principles; spontaneous and obvious knowledge is contested, undermined, broken-up and contradicted one fragment at a time and replaced with Professional Consensus (Peer Review).

*

What does PC put in the place of The Good, and its component transcendentals of Virtue, Beauty and Truth?

Thought Prison

Nothing definite – because for PC there is no reality.

Instead there are an infinite number of relative 'realities'.

PC subverts The Good, but offers no substitute for The Good – except The *Better*.

The Good versus The Better

PC does not know what it aims-for; it knows only that it must destroy The Good, that it may be replaced by something Better – only it has no criteria for evaluating what is Better than Good – only that the Better be *different* from what is.

Since evaluations are themselves relative for PC, the Better can never really be *known* to be Better than the Good, but the belief is that the (earthly) Good is certainly not perfect, and by change it *might become* Better…

PC therefore subverts the Good and seeks the Better; in belief (or hope) that the Better will *emerge* as a consequence of the evolving process.

If PC has any faith, which is doubtful, it is that this *evolutionary* process of subversion and experiment is *intrinsically* virtuous.

*

This is how it works:

Current and past realities always have specific flaws when compared with an ideal.

(Some of these specific flaws of reality loom very large to moderns, such as that all human societies before 1800 accepted slavery.)

Since there are an infinite number of *imaginable* alternative realities which have all the desirable attributes of real history but lack these specific flaws, it follows that there "must be" many potential realities, among which some "must be" *Better* than any current or past reality.

*

The job of PC is then to destroy current reality, detach itself from all past realities, and seek among the infinity of alternatives for something Better (which "must"– surely? – be there, by sheer mathematical probability).

PC will sort-through, experiment-with these alternative realities to find something Better – maybe something *perfect*?

(Anyone who opposes this virtuous process of search and experiment, is regarded simply as an apologist for the specific evils of the present and the past. In a nutshell: to prefer the past is to advocate slavery.)

*

When PC subverts The Good and instead promotes Vice, Lies, and Ugliness this is self-perceived as merely *humble experiments in pursuit of the Better*.

Can the desire to end suffering be the primary motivation?

The most frequently-expressed Leftist political goal is to end human suffering in the world – or at least minimize it.

This carries force, since we are creatures of this world, as well as being motivated by a desire to attain pleasure we want *even more* to escape suffering, and empathically to relieve suffering (which makes us suffer too).

*

So long as we *perceive* suffering in the world – even if that suffering is just insufficient pleasure or mere boredom – then we will be motivated (to some extent) to end it.

Indeed, we are motivated (to some extent) to end suffering everywhere and for everyone for all time – simply as a matter of security.

Because so long as suffering happens *somewhere* to *someone* – or may do so in future – then it *could* happen to us!

But if there is no more suffering *at all*, then we need never fear it, whatever happens...

*

But suppose (as a thought experiment) that all suffering has indeed been ended (at least *so far as we know*).

What then? Do we imagine that *when* all suffering has been ended *then* we will shift our aspiration to *higher* things?

Or that *only when* all suffering had been ended *ought* we to shift our aspiration to higher things?

Do we really think that is what did, and should, and would happen?

*

Is this, in fact, what we observe?

Are the societies that suffer least, those which aspire the highest?

Are those historic societies which attained the highest levels of holiness also those societies where life was most comfortable?

Are those individuals who are free-est from suffering, also those individuals who have their sights set on the highest ideals?

*

Do we, in a word, conceive high ideals as *luxury goods*?

*

Or could it be that high ideals are, in some way or another, a *product* of suffering – or, if not exactly suffering, of a state of discontent?

Um – yes, that is correct. Isn't it?

It is our suffering that prompts us to look beyond the mundane.

(Prompts us – but does not *force* us.)

*

Is suffering then good?

Obviously *not*.

As worldly creatures we are, and must be, motivated to escape suffering in some sense.

But suffering is – if not good – surely *necessary* or at least *inevitable* in this world.

*

And – surely? – a *primary* devotion to the elimination of suffering (i.e. the new religion, the new 'Christianity' indeed) is therefore not merely Utopian or futile – but is actually *evil*. Is indeed, actually a covert death wish (death being, for atheists, the only sure end to suffering) – and perhaps a deep cause of the anti-life malaise so characteristic of political correctness.

The world is not enough

We *just are* creatures who perceive the world as insufficient.

And the only way we can get rid of this perception is to kill it.

*

We cannot make the world sufficient, we can only destroy the perception that the world is insufficient.

But we *can* do that: for most of the people, for most of the time.

And that is, of course, precisely what we are doing.

*

Indeed, although we are, and must be, and should not try not to be, creatures of this world; a primary devotion directed at anything of this world (including the elimination of suffering) is evil.

Our primary devotion should be to The Good – the transcendental Good, a something *not* of this world. Or else we (and everyone else) might as well be dead already, or (even-better) never live in the first place – as the surest means of avoiding suffering...

Just as we 'put down' a suffering animal; whom we suppose *not* to have a soul, and whose role is to serve humans and/ or be happy – and if the animal can no longer serve humans nor be happy and is suffering, then it might as well be dead – so we kill it.

Then (by modern secular reasoning) to eliminate suffering we also *ought to* kill anything else we suppose *not* to have a soul – and do so from *humane* motives.

If suffering is regarded the worst evil (as modern secularism believes), and if death is extinction (as soul-denying PC believes) then *universal death is logically the greatest good* – an end to all conscious life including suicide is then the only sure ethical policy.

*

Political correctness believes that humans, like animals, lack a soul – and believes that death is an end to consciousness. PC also believes that suffering is the worst evil.

That combination should worry you.

Can't we simply subtract PC from modernity?

Political correctness is generally talked-of as a *factor* in modern society; but it is primarily a *spiritual malaise*. PC is not so much a 'factor' as simply the entire world view of mainstream modern Western intellectuals (Left, Right and Centre).

Since PC is pervasive, whatever the future holds, one future we *cannot* have (even if we really wanted it, and tried to get it – which we don't and aren't) is to have modern society without political correctness.

*

We cannot have the stuff which makes modern life so stimulating and comfortable *minus* PC.

Yet of course, on the other hand, we cannot have the stuff which makes modern life so stimulating and comfortable *with* PC; because PC is both actively and passively destroying all of these.

So… we are *going to lose* modern society whatever happens – whether PC continues and destroys these things, or whether PC is itself destroyed and replaced.

From the stimulation and comfort perspective, it is a lose-lose situation.

*

Lack of common sense will be the end of PC, yet political correctness cannot save itself with a dose of common sense because *PC cannot yield an inch in the direction of common sense*: since from where PC has landed-us common sense will take us directly to something very like fascism; something which is utterly opposed (and not by accident) to everything which PC stands-for – including a life dedicated to stimulation and comfort.

*

And we cannot go back to any point earlier in modernity, since these were merely *transitional eras* when PC had not *quite* broken through to dominance; but it was there, and all trends were set for it to take-over.

It would be futile to try, but we cannot even try; because there are no grounds for leverage.

That is, to exert pressure for change we would need to get outside PC sufficiently to exert leverage against PC.

Yet so long as we remain within Western modernity, we are still within PC, and not outside of it.

There is nowhere from which to operate a lever.

PC and 'original sin'

The special quality of PC, compared with secular Right wing politics, is that it retains from earlier religious cultural stages a core belief in what might be termed a secular version of Original Sin (the ultimate, inborn selfishness and inevitable corruptibility of human beings) and feels intense guilt for this, and this guilt cannot be divinely forgiven so propitiation must be made *within this world.*

*

So, whereas communism believed that human beings were perfectible, since the perfect society would, according to communism, yield perfect humans who made virtuous choices without coercion – PC by contrast believes that humans are necessarily selfish and corruptible: that humans cannot be trusted, *ever*: humans will always tend to choose selfishly.

And therefore, for PC the perfect society must be structured such that human choice is eliminated.

*

This insight into the sinfulness of human nature is the source from which political correctness draws its ideological strength; because the insight that humans are necessarily selfish and corruptible is indeed *true.*

Therefore political correctness is based upon a *deeper perception of reality* than its secular Right opponents - who often try to argue that humans are 'not-all-that-bad', or not all of them, anyway.

Well, actually, humans *are* that bad!

*

But that is not the end of the matter.

The big question is not to quibble over the spontaneously recognized fact that humans are fundamentally sinful, but what are the *implications* of the fact.

That humans are sinful, that there is something fundamentally *wrong* with us, and that we ought rightly to feel guilt, have been truisms of religious insight for as long as we have records.

There is therefore nothing *new* about PC regarding humans as sinful and guilty – that is not a novelty of PC in any way shape or form.

But what *is* new about PC is what to do about 'original sin'.

Faith in abstract systems

What is new about PC is the *response* to perceiving the sinfulness of humans.

The only solution to intrinsic human sin and guilt is faith in the reality of non-human 'salvation'.

*

Traditional religion, perceiving humanity to be sinful, located goodness in the non-material, transcendental or supernatural world. So that in Christianity, The Good was located in God.

But for PC there is neither God nor anything existing outside either the meaningless material realm and the sinful realm of human subjectivity.

Therefore PC locates moral virtue in a non-human *and also* non-material realm: *the realm of abstract system*.

*

Here is an important difference between the majority of unreflective, careerist and opportunistic PC drones and the inner elite of self-aware, moral and devoutly-PC:

The careerist PC masses locate sin in Right-wingers

But the devout PC elite recognize the sinfulness of *all* humans.

The careerist PC masses seek a solution in replacing rulership of the sinful Right with rulership of the virtuous Left.

But the devout PC elite seek a solution not in replacing one gang of sinful humans with another gang (who are, ultimately, just as bad); but in replacing *all human agency in all circumstances with abstract systems* – even their own agency.

The sincerely and truly-PC seek to subordinate everyone *including themselves* to abstract systems.

*

The replacement for individual agency is currently almost always one form of systemic formal bureaucracy or another: committee decision, peer review, voting, algorithms, flow-charts, protocols, guidelines, quotas...

Tactically, it doesn't really matter which of these, or others, are implemented because all are more abstract and less personal than individual agency.

For PC these are all a step in the right direction.

*

Since formal bureaucracy is all pervasive and authoritative in Western modernity, so is political correctness all pervasive and authoritative – PC may be weird, irrational, suicidal to common sense – but PC is *main*stream*;* even in its *ex*tremes.

Mainstream modern public discourse is therefore politically correct; mainstream discussion occurs only and always between *degrees* of political correctness; between the more-PC and the less-PC, between *avant garde* and traditional PC – but all public discourse is PC.

129

*

The mainstream Right (Conservative, Republican, Libertarian etc.) is therefore nowadays, always, fundamentally and necessarily politically correct.

For example, the mainstream Right often locates virtue not in individuals but in abstract systems (competition, the market, the outcome of the Open Society, the Constitution etc).

The disagreement between the libertarian Right and the liberal Left is often merely a minor *quibble* over what kind of abstract system is preferable, and how it is to be implemented.

We are all politically-correct now!

*

This is why PC cannot be defeated by any existing strand of public discourse – all influential public discourse (Right and Left) is fundamentally PC in its assumptions, and differs only in degree.

This is why there is no possibility of de-converting the PC elite – there is nobody to de-convert them!

(And the PC elites will resist any common sense reforms as tending-towards-fascism: and they would be correct in inferring this tendency.)

PC can only be replaced, not reformed.

Why don't you convert to political correctness?

So...

Since you can't do anything about political correctness, why not just make the *best* of it?

Why not *exploit* the situation instead of moaning about it?

Do what is *expedient* – why not?

*

Why not make a successful *career* out of PC – like so many others?

Why not surrender your private mind to PC, in the same way as you have already surrendered your public behaviour?

By having any reservations at all, you are making yourself miserable – why not simply cast-aside those reservations?

Just say an inner *yes* to what you will, anyway, be forced to do...

*

Since you necessarily inhabit the thought prison that is political correctness – then why not, at least, become one of the 'trustys' among the inmates – to assist with the smooth running of the gaol, and get yourself a few privileges.

Why not, indeed, strive to become one of the guards? Somebody has to do the job! Maybe you could temper the severity of the regime?

And herein lies the *particular temptation* for the intellectual elite – a temptation few resist.

*

That (literally) soul-destroying pragmatism by which (for eminently *sensible* reasons) we quietly, by gradual degrees, *change sides* in the spiritual battle of the world: that unseen warfare between The Good and that which opposes The Good.

Well why not?

There is no *earthly* reason why not.

In a world of pervasive and powerful PC, there is really only *one* compelling reason for holding back and resisting in any way, shape or form – which is that embracing political correctness will *damage your soul*.

*

If you do *not* believe in the soul, this reason will carry no force at all: so by your own calculations you are stupid to resist PC.

Or, if you believe the soul is inviolable, and that nothing you think or do can affect the soul: then also, by your own calculations, you are stupid to resist PC.

132

If you do not believe in Natural Law (innate knowledge of The Good), and that breaking Natural Law harms the soul: then logically you should learn to love PC.

*

If you do not believe in the reality of the transcendental Good – then you might as well go with the flow, allow yourself to be re-programmed: to learn, by regular practice, to re-label lies as truth, ugliness as beauty, evil as virtue; until PC has entered into your heart, as well as pouring into your ears and out-from your mouth.

*

Political correctness is nihilism; therefore it is not merely political: it is existential.

To fight against political correctness is ultimately an existential act: a battle to preserve the eternal soul.

*

But if you do *not* believe that political correctness will harm your eternal soul: then you would be well-advised to suck it up.

Why not?...

How to be non-PC

Since the entire modern institutional mainstream is essentially politically correct, then to be non-PC you need to be cut-off from the mainstream.

At the least you need to make sacrifices; specifically to forgo aspirations towards mainstream power and status; and if you do so, then, unless embedded in a traditional orthodox religious society (and if you are, then you won't be reading these words), you will be more or less *on your own*.

*

To be non-PC is not, therefore, a matter of building a political movement; it is a matter of personal salvation – done, not with hope of changing the world by worldly methods, but because you ought to do it.

*

To reject PC is fraught with its own hazards: going-off-the-rails due to lack of external guidance; falling into self-conceit and arrogance; the terrible sin of spiritual pride.

However, lacking any non-PC institutional support network, there is no real alternative for most people to 'going solo'.

*

So, how to reject PC, lacking public support – and indeed in the face of almost monolithically hostile pro-PC discourse and a world view based upon deep premises which cannot be challenged but which lead inexorably to PC?

Some of the answer is simple –

Negatively, a mixture of avoiding (as much as possible) participation in the mass media, and avoiding (as much as possible) the discourse of high level modern bureaucracy; and

Positively, an immersion (as much as possible) in traditional non-PC discourse (which will necessarily mostly be written, and from the historical sources, and from an 'orthodox' religious perspective).

*

And that's it!

Postscript

That's it.

Except, of course, that *tradition* is borne not by the written word, but by its interpretation; therefore by humans.

On that basis we haven't got a chance, since the thread of tradition has been broken, and there are no (or almost no) wise and adept non-PC spiritual advisers.

But then there is the hope of *external* help, from outside of the human world, by praying for the Grace to understand and the strength to choose.

Ultimately, that is what we must rely upon.

However, if you personally don't believe in the *possibility* of external help, then I'm afraid you have *no* legitimate grounds for hope – but you will instead simply have to hope for hope…

Note to the reader

This book is intended for normal, mainstream, secular, modern, disaffected and alienated intellectuals; those who are complicit in political correctness (as are all intellectuals) but who are (when not distracted, drugged or dreaming) in a state of despair.

This book will, I hope, help such people to understand their condition, and present the likely choices. It will not help them to save their world (too late for that) but it may help them to save their souls.